NATIONAL SECURITY

Opposing Viewpoints®

Helen Cothran, *Book Editor*

Daniel Leone, *President*
Bonnie Szumski, *Publisher*
Scott Barbour, *Managing Editor*

OPPOSING
VIEWPOINTS®
SERIES

GREENHAVEN
PRESS®

THOMSON
━━━━━★━━━━━ ™
GALE

San Diego • Detroit • New York • San Francisco • Cleveland
New Haven, Conn. • Waterville, Maine • London • Munich

LIBRARY OF CONGRESS CATALOGING-IN-PUBLICATION DATA

National security : opposing viewpoints / Helen Cothran, book editor.
    p. cm. — (Opposing viewpoints series)
Includes bibliographical references and index.
ISBN 0-7377-1696-7 (pbk. : alk. paper) — ISBN 0-7377-1695-9 (lib. : alk. paper)
    1. National security—United States. 2. United States—Defenses.
3. Terrorism—United States—Prevention. 4. War on Terrorism, 2001– .
I. Cothran, Helen. II. Opposing viewpoints series (Unnumbered)
UA234.N2476 2004
355'.033073—dc21
                                      2003044862

Printed in the United States of America

"Congress shall make no law. . . abridging the freedom of speech, or of the press."

First Amendment to the U.S. Constitution

The basic foundation of our democracy is the First Amendment guarantee of freedom of expression. The Opposing Viewpoints Series is dedicated to the concept of this basic freedom and the idea that it is more important to practice it than to enshrine it.

Contents

Why Consider Opposing Viewpoints?

"The only way in which a human being can make some approach to knowing the whole of a subject is by hearing what can be said about it by persons of every variety of opinion and studying all modes in which it can be looked at by every character of mind. No wise man ever acquired his wisdom in any mode but this."

John Stuart Mill

In our media-intensive culture it is not difficult to find differing opinions. Thousands of newspapers and magazines and dozens of radio and television talk shows resound with differing points of view. The difficulty lies in deciding which opinion to agree with and which "experts" seem the most credible. The more inundated we become with differing opinions and claims, the more essential it is to hone critical reading and thinking skills to evaluate these ideas. Opposing Viewpoints books address this problem directly by presenting stimulating debates that can be used to enhance and teach these skills. The varied opinions contained in each book examine many different aspects of a single issue. While examining these conveniently edited opposing views, readers can develop critical thinking skills such as the ability to compare and contrast authors' credibility, facts, argumentation styles, use of persuasive techniques, and other stylistic tools. In short, the Opposing Viewpoints Series is an ideal way to attain the higher-level thinking and reading skills so essential in a culture of diverse and contradictory opinions.

In addition to providing a tool for critical thinking, Opposing Viewpoints books challenge readers to question their own strongly held opinions and assumptions. Most people form their opinions on the basis of upbringing, peer pressure, and personal, cultural, or professional bias. By reading carefully balanced opposing views, readers must directly confront new ideas as well as the opinions of those with whom they disagree. This is not to simplistically argue that

everyone who reads opposing views will—or should—
change his or her opinion. Instead, the series enhances readers' understanding of their own views by encouraging confrontation with opposing ideas. Careful examination of others' views can lead to the readers' understanding of the
logical inconsistencies in their own opinions, perspective on
why they hold an opinion, and the consideration of the possibility that their opinion requires further evaluation.

Evaluating Other Opinions

To ensure that this type of examination occurs, Opposing
Viewpoints books present all types of opinions. Prominent
spokespeople on different sides of each issue as well as well-
known professionals from many disciplines challenge the
reader. An additional goal of the series is to provide a forum
for other, less known, or even unpopular viewpoints. The
opinion of an ordinary person who has had to make the decision to cut off life support from a terminally ill relative, for
example, may be just as valuable and provide just as much insight as a medical ethicist's professional opinion. The editors
have two additional purposes in including these less known
views. One, the editors encourage readers to respect others'
opinions—even when not enhanced by professional credibility. It is only by reading or listening to and objectively evaluating others' ideas that one can determine whether they are
worthy of consideration. Two, the inclusion of such viewpoints encourages the important critical thinking skill of objectively evaluating an author's credentials and bias. This
evaluation will illuminate an author's reasons for taking a
particular stance on an issue and will aid in readers' evaluation of the author's ideas.

It is our hope that these books will give readers a deeper
understanding of the issues debated and an appreciation of
the complexity of even seemingly simple issues when good
and honest people disagree. This awareness is particularly
important in a democratic society such as ours in which
people enter into public debate to determine the common
good. Those with whom one disagrees should not be regarded as enemies but rather as people whose views deserve
careful examination and may shed light on one's own.

Thomas Jefferson once said that "difference of opinion leads to inquiry, and inquiry to truth." Jefferson, a broadly educated man, argued that "if a nation expects to be ignorant and free . . . it expects what never was and never will be." As individuals and as a nation, it is imperative that we consider the opinions of others and examine them with skill and discernment. The Opposing Viewpoints Series is intended to help readers achieve this goal.

David L. Bender and Bruno Leone,
Founders

Greenhaven Press anthologies primarily consist of previously published material taken from a variety of sources, including periodicals, books, scholarly journals, newspapers, government documents, and position papers from private and public organizations. These original sources are often edited for length and to ensure their accessibility for a young adult audience. The anthology editors also change the original titles of these works in order to clearly present the main thesis of each viewpoint and to explicitly indicate the opinion presented in the viewpoint. These alterations are made in consideration of both the reading and comprehension levels of a young adult audience. Every effort is made to ensure that Greenhaven Press accurately reflects the original intent of the authors included in this anthology.

Introduction

"While there is still tremendous support for the U.S. [war against terrorism], countries aren't just going to be cheerleaders while we do whatever we want."
—*James B. Steinberg, director of the Foreign Policy Studies Program at the Brookings Institution*

In the days following the September 11, 2001, terrorist attacks on America, countries from around the world denounced the attacks. Traditional foes such as Russia publicly expressed sympathy while long-standing allies such as Canada, Great Britain, Australia, and France pledged their support in finding and prosecuting those responsible. This global outpouring of sympathy gave U.S. officials reason to hope that they could count on the international community to help fight terrorism. However, as the United States began to execute its war on terrorism in the months following September 11, international support began to diminish. Although President George W. Bush seemed determined to continue the war without the help of allies, critics of his stance argued that America's security would depend upon the relationships it nurtured with other nations.

As the forces of globalization change the economic, political, and social relationships between nations, the geographic bulwarks that America counted on to protect it are proving insufficient. Two oceans and two friendly neighbors may help protect a nation from invasion but do little to thwart terrorists. Advances in information technologies have, in essence, shrunk the distances between countries, allowing people to conduct business from anywhere on the globe. Such advances made it possible for the September 11 terrorists to coordinate the attack from various nations. Globalization has also led to an increase in tourism and travel, making it easier for terrorists to hide in host countries without drawing attention. All nineteen of the September 11 terrorists came to the United States on legal visas, and several overstayed them without drawing the notice of U.S. security agencies.

In addition to globalization, other changes have affected

America's security. With the Cold War over, America's enemies have changed. Some of the most serious threats to national security are no longer established nation-states such as Russia but terrorist groups such as al-Qaeda, the group responsible for the September 11 attacks. During the Cold War, security was in large part a matter of outspending enemies on military hardware and sending American spies to the Kremlin. Such Cold War methods have proven ineffective in combating loosely organized terrorist groups scattered all over the globe. As became evident after September 11, the largest military in the world cannot prevent terrorists from flying commercial airplanes into buildings. Moreover, CIA operatives who can speak Russian are of little help in infiltrating terrorist cells in Afghanistan.

In the post–Cold War era, with globalization making national borders more porous, America's reliance on shear strength to keep enemies at bay has come under increased scrutiny. Professor Janice Gross Stein asserts, "Military preeminence, no matter how overwhelming, does not buy the United States security from attack, even in its heartland." In light of this fact, as Stein puts it, the nation needs to "acknowledge the need for multilateral solutions." Without the help of its friends, many analysts argue, the United States will find itself isolated. Henry Kissinger, national security adviser and later secretary of state under former presidents Richard Nixon and Gerald Ford, asserts, "The United States will not be able to sort out every international problem alone without exhausting itself physically and psychologically." Therefore, he concludes, "the ultimate challenge for American foreign policy is to turn dominant power into a sense of shared responsibility." By nurturing international alliances, these analysts assert, America can help create a unified front against terrorism.

Despite arguments for multilateralism, the Bush administration early on illustrated its willingness to go it alone in fighting America's enemies. Although Bush was successful in gaining the help of allies to fight the war in Afghanistan to rout the Taliban, the ruling regime that had sponsored al-Qaeda, further actions extending the war on terrorism met with international resistance. As the United States contemplated an invasion of Iraq in an attempt to neutralize the threat posed by

Iraqi leader Saddam Hussein, who purportedly helped al-Qaeda carry out the September 11 attacks, America's allies balked. Many argued that the use of preemptive strikes against Iraq would violate the United Nations (UN) Charter, which prohibits signatories from using aggression against another nation unless for self-defense. Such a lack of international support did not discourage Bush, however, who illustrated a partiality toward unilateralism early in his administration.

One example of Bush's willingness to pursue America's interests in the face of international protest is his endorsement of a national missile defense system—a shield that would protect the homeland from ballistic missiles. However, pursuing such a system would violate the Anti-Ballistic Missile Treaty (ABM), the international arms control agreement responsible for slowing nuclear proliferation. The international community voiced strong opposition to U.S. withdrawal from the treaty, but Bush elected to withdraw anyway. As professor Stein puts it, "More and more, the U.S. is insisting on an exception for itself from the rules that govern others." However, many U.S. presidents besides Bush have viewed international agreements such as the ABM Treaty as restrictive and ultimately serving the needs of other nations at the expense of America's security.

At the heart of the debate about national security is the question of how much the safety of the United States depends on its relationships with other nations. Those who minimize this dependency are confident that America's military superiority can guarantee its security with minimal help from other nations. Others argue that force alone is not enough. They believe that post–Cold War era threats demand more coalition building. The authors in *National Security: Opposing Viewpoints* debate many of the methods now being considered and implemented to enhance the nation's safety in the following chapters: What Are the Most Serious Threats to National Security? How Can National Security Best Be Enhanced? How Should the United States Respond to Terrorism? Do Efforts to Enhance National Security Threaten Civil Liberties? One thing is certain: The threats facing America have changed, and the nation will have to adopt new approaches to combating them if it is to avoid another September 11.

CHAPTER 1

What Are the Most Serious Threats to National Security?

Chapter Preface

The unusual nature of the September 11, 2001, terrorist attacks on America (no one had ever intentionally flown commercial airplanes into buildings before) jarred the nation's security experts from complacency. In a matter of hours, their notions about what constituted the most serious threats to the nation's security were shattered. Realizing that old thinking about conventional threats would no longer suffice, they quickly began to predict new threats. One threat immediately came to the fore: Terrorists could intentionally crash a commercial airliner into one of America's 103 operating nuclear power plants.

Intense debate has exploded over whether or not a commercial airliner could seriously damage the containment shell of a nuclear reactor. Reactors were designed to withstand attacks by small planes and vehicles filled with explosives, but no one had envisioned terrorists crashing an airliner into a plant. Still, because reactors are protected by sixteen feet of concrete and other safety measures, most experts doubt that they would be primary targets for terrorists. Steve Kerekes, spokesman for the Nuclear Energy Institute, claims, "Our reactors are as well protected as anything you're going to find." Far more vulnerable are the spent fuel repositories at plant sites.

Spent fuel pools—the nearly forty-foot-deep reservoirs that house depleted nuclear fuel—are not protected by thick concrete domes. In fact, most of the spent fuel pools are contained in standard aboveground concrete or corrugated buildings. Plant designers originally planned to have spent fuel transported to special federal repositories, but as yet no repository sites have been approved. In consequence, nearly forty thousand tons of spent fuel are now being stored at reactor sites. If terrorists could destroy the structure holding the water that cools the radioactive rods, the rods could ignite. The resulting fire would release cesium-137, potentially causing hundreds of thousands of cancer deaths and rendering hundreds of square miles of land uninhabitable for generations.

After the September 11 attacks, officials have rushed to

enhance security at nuclear power plants throughout the nation. Planes have been banned from the airspace above the facilities, and the National Guard and Coast Guard have begun patrolling their perimeters. More security agents are now working at the plants, and physical barriers have been erected at entrance points. In addition, new employees must have their background checks approved before they can begin work, and new employees' names are now cross-checked with the FBI's suspected terrorist list. Notwithstanding these precautions, many of those concerned about safety argue that the nuclear power industry's track record on making safety a priority fails to instill confidence. Massachusetts representative Edward J. Markey, who has criticized the Nuclear Regulatory Commission for years about safety issues, contends, "These plants were flunking elementary school security exams, and complaining the whole time that the exams were too hard. Well, they need to start passing college-level tests. Now."

In the aftermath of a serious terrorist attack on the nation's soil, some overreaction concerning security risks is natural. Industry officials are quick to claim that the threat from a nuclear disaster at one of their plants has been greatly exaggerated. Still, the unexpected nature of the September 11 attacks taught Americans that the unthinkable can happen. In the following chapter, authors discuss other threats to the nation's security. The challenge ahead for security officials across the country is to correctly identify which threats are most serious and then decide how to use the nation's limited resources to combat them.

"Terrorist groups worldwide have ready access to information on chemical, biological, and even nuclear weapons via the Internet."

Terrorism Is a Serious Threat to National Security

George J. Tenet

In the following viewpoint, originally delivered as a speech before the Senate Armed Services Committee on March 19, 2002, George J. Tenet claims that despite many successes in fighting terrorism following the September 11, 2001, terrorist attacks, the United States must not relax its guard against terrorists. According to Tenet, the terrorist threat will likely grow as terrorist groups acquire weapons of mass destruction to use against the United States. The threat will also increase, he maintains, because growing domestic unrest and conflict in weak nations will foster an environment conducive to terrorism. Tenet asserts that the United States must not focus all of its attention on Muslim nations in the Middle East but must watch other countries from which terrorists are planning attacks against America. Tenet is the director of the Central Intelligence Agency.

As you read, consider the following questions:
1. Why is Tenet concerned about Somalia?
2. What is a "dirty bomb," according to the author?
3. As reported by Tenet, how many al-Qaeda extremists have been arrested since the September 11, 2001, terrorist attacks?

George J. Tenet, "Worldwide Threat: Converging Dangers in a Post 9/11 World," testimony before the Senate Armed Services Committee, March 19, 2002.

M r. Chairman, I appear before you this year [2002] under circumstances that are extraordinary and historic for reasons I need not recount. Never before has the subject of this annual threat briefing had more immediate resonance. Never before have the dangers been more clear or more present.

Converging Threats

[The September 11, 2001, terrorist attacks] brought together and brought home—literally—several vital threats to the United States and its interests that we have long been aware of. It is the convergence of these threats that I want to emphasize with you today: the connection between terrorists and other enemies of this country; the weapons of mass destruction they seek to use against us; and the social, economic, and political tensions across the world that they exploit in mobilizing their followers. September 11 demonstrated the dangers that arise when these threats converge—and it reminds us that we overlook at our own peril the impact of crises in remote parts of the world.

This convergence of threats has created the world I will present to you today—a world in which dangers exist not only in those places where we have most often focused our attention, but also in other areas that demand it:

- In places like Somalia, where the absence of a national government has created an environment in which groups sympathetic to al-Qa'ida [the terrorist group responsible for the September 11 attacks] have offered terrorists an operational base and potential haven.
- In places like Indonesia, where political instability, separatist and ethnic tensions, and protracted violence are hampering economic recovery and fueling Islamic extremism.
- In places like Colombia, where leftist insurgents who make much of their money from drug trafficking are escalating their assault on the government—further undermining economic prospects and fueling a cycle of violence.
- And finally, Mr. Chairman, in places like Connecticut, where the death of a 94-year-old woman in her own

home of anthrax poisoning can arouse our worst fears about what our enemies might try to do to us.

These threats demand our utmost response. The United States has clearly demonstrated since September 11 that it is up to the challenge. But make no mistake: despite the battles we have won in Afghanistan [in routing the Taliban, the ruling regime that harbored al-Qa'ida], we remain a nation at war.

The Most Immediate and Serious Threats

Last year I told you that [terrorist] Usama Bin Ladin and the al-Qa'ida network were the most immediate and serious threat this country faced. This remains true today despite the progress we have made in Afghanistan and in disrupting the network elsewhere. We assess that al-Qa'ida and other terrorist groups will continue to plan to attack this country and its interests abroad. Their modus operandi is to have multiple attack plans in the works simultaneously, and to have al-Qa'ida cells in place to conduct them.

- We know that terrorists have considered attacks in the US against high-profile government or private facilities, famous landmarks, and US infrastructure nodes such as airports, bridges, harbors, dams, and financial centers.
- American diplomatic and military installations are at high risk—especially in East Africa, Israel, Saudi Arabia, Turkey, Pakistan, and Afghanistan.
- Operations against US targets could be launched by al-Qa'ida cells already in place in major cities in Europe and the Middle East. Al-Qa'ida can also exploit its presence or connections to other groups in such countries as Somalia, Yemen, Indonesia, and the Philippines.

Weapons of Mass Destruction

Although the September 11 attacks suggest that al-Qa'ida and other terrorists will continue to use conventional weapons, one of our highest concerns is their stated readiness to attempt unconventional attacks against us. As early as 1998, Bin Ladin publicly declared that acquiring unconventional weapons was "a religious duty."

- Terrorist groups worldwide have ready access to information on chemical, biological, and even nuclear weapons via the Internet, and we know that al-Qa'ida was working to acquire some of the most dangerous chemical agents and toxins. Documents recovered from al-Qa'ida facilities in Afghanistan show that Bin Ladin was pursuing a sophisticated biological weapons research program.

- We also believe that Bin Ladin was seeking to acquire or develop a nuclear device. Al-Qa'ida may be pursuing a radioactive dispersal device—what some call a "dirty bomb."
- Alternatively, al-Qa'ida or other terrorist groups might try to launch conventional attacks against the chemical or nuclear industrial infrastructure of the United States to cause widespread toxic or radiological damage.

We are also alert to the possibility of cyber warfare attack by terrorists. September 11 demonstrated our dependence on critical infrastructure systems that rely on electronic and computer networks. Attacks of this nature will become an increasingly viable option for terrorists as they and other foreign adversaries become more familiar with these targets, and the technologies required to attack them.

A Multitude of Threats

The terrorist threat in the Muslim world goes well beyond al-Qa'ida. The situation in the Middle East continues to fuel terrorism and anti-US sentiment worldwide. Groups like the Palestine Islamic Jihad (PIJ) and HAMAS have escalated their violence against Israel, and the intifadah [holy war] has rejuvenated once-dormant groups like the Popular Front for the Liberation of Palestine. If these groups feel that US actions are threatening their existence, they may begin targeting Americans directly.

- The terrorist threat also goes beyond Islamic extremists and the Muslim world. The Revolutionary Armed Forces of Colombia (FARC) poses a serious threat to US interests in Latin America because it associates us with the government it is fighting against.
- The same is true in Turkey, where the Revolutionary People's Liberation Party/Front has publicly criticized the United States and our operations in Afghanistan.

19

Cyberterrorism

During the past several years, military officials have become concerned about the possibility that a foreign adversary might strike at U.S. computers, communications networks, and databases. Although such an "information warfare" (IW) attack could be part of a larger conventional military operation, an adversary might also use it as a warning shot to dissuade the United States from helping an ally abroad or as part of a terrorist campaign.

IW presents special problems for defense planners. Many, if not most, targets of such an attack would probably be commercial computer and communications systems, which are more vulnerable than those operated by the military. Yet commercial operators are seemingly unaware that they are potential targets, and few have taken any precautionary measures. Most software and hardware designers are also not attuned to the IW threat.

Bruce Berkowitz, *World & I*, January 2002.

We are also watching states like Iran and Iraq that continue to support terrorist groups.

- Iran continues to provide support—including arms transfers—to Palestinian rejectionist groups and Hizballah. Tehran has also failed to move decisively against al-Qa'ida members who have relocated to Iran from Afghanistan.
- Iraq has a long history of supporting terrorists, including giving sanctuary to [terrorist] Abu Nidal.

Mr. Chairman, while al-Qa'ida represents a broad-based Sunni worldwide extremist network, it would be a mistake to dismiss possible connections to either other groups or state sponsors—either Sunni or Shia [two different Muslim sects]. There is a convergence of common interest in hurting the US, its allies, and interests that make traditional thinking in this regard unacceptable.

Making Inroads Against Terrorism

The war on terrorism has dealt severe blows to al-Qa'ida and its leadership. The group is no longer able to run large-scale training and recruitment programs in Afghanistan. Drawing on both our own assets and increased cooperation from allies around the world, we are uncovering terrorists' plans and breaking up their cells. These efforts have yielded the arrest of over 1,300 extremists believed to be associated with al-Qa'ida operatives in over 70 countries, and have disrupted terrorist operations and potential terrorist attacks.

Mr. Chairman, Bin Ladin did not believe that we would invade his sanctuary. He saw the United States as soft, impatient, unprepared, and fearful of a long, bloody war of attrition. He did not count on the fact that we had lined up allies that could help us overcome barriers of terrain and culture. He did not know about the collection and operational initiatives that would allow us to strike—with great accuracy—at the heart of the Taliban and al-Qa'ida. He underestimated our capabilities, our readiness, and our resolve.

That said, I must repeat that al-Qa'ida has not yet been destroyed. It and other like-minded groups remain willing and able to strike us. Al-Qa'ida leaders still at large are working to reconstitute the organization and to resume its terrorist operations. We must eradicate these organizations by denying them their sources of financing and eliminating their ability to hijack charitable organizations for their terrorist purposes. We must be prepared for a long war, and we must not falter.

Mr. Chairman, we must also look beyond the immediate danger of terrorist attacks to the conditions that allow terrorism to take root around the world. These conditions are no less threatening to US national security than terrorism itself. The problems that terrorists exploit—poverty, alienation, and ethnic tensions—will grow more acute over the next decade. This will especially be the case in those parts of the world that have served as the most fertile recruiting grounds for Islamic extremist groups.

- We have already seen—in Afghanistan and elsewhere— that domestic unrest and conflict in weak states is one of the factors that create an environment conducive to terrorism.
- More importantly, demographic trends tell us that the world's poorest and most politically unstable regions— which include parts of the Middle East and Sub-Saharan Africa—will have the largest youth populations in the

world over the next two decades and beyond. Most of these countries will lack the economic institutions or resources to effectively integrate these youth into society. . . .

A Commitment to Fight Terrorism

Mr. Chairman, I want to end my presentation by reaffirming what the President [George W. Bush] has said on many occasions regarding the threats we face from terrorists and other adversaries. We cannot—and will not—relax our guard against these enemies. If we did so, the terrorists would have won. And that will not happen. The terrorists, rather, should stand warned that we will not falter in our efforts, and in our commitment, until the threat they pose to us has been eliminated.

"Frequent repetition of . . . stories [about terrorist threats] may lead people to overestimate the likelihood of future dire events."

The Terrorist Threat Has Been Exaggerated

Michael L. Rothschild

Michael L. Rothschild argues in the following viewpoint that the steady stream of media stories about terrorist threats following the September 11, 2001, terrorist attacks has caused people to overestimate the risk that terrorists pose to Americans' security. He claims that Americans have a greater chance of dying in an automobile accident or from heart disease than they do of being killed by a terrorist. This exaggerated sense of personal danger has led many Americans to avoid public places such as malls, which has resulted in high economic costs, Rothschild contends. Michael L. Rothschild is an emeritus professor at the University of Wisconsin's business school.

As you read, consider the following questions:

1. What are the odds of dying in an automobile accident as compared to being killed by a terrorist in a mall, as cited by the author?
2. According to Rothschild, how do people tend to estimate the risk of a rare event occurring?
3. How did residents of Madison, Wisconsin, react to anthrax-related news stories, as reported by the author?

Michael L. Rothschild, "Terrorism and You: The Real Odds," *Washington Post*, vol. 19, December 3, 2001, p. 27. Copyright © 2001 by Michael L. Rothschild. Reproduced by permission.

The odds of dying in an automobile accident each year are about one in 7,000, yet we continue to drive. The odds of dying from heart disease in any given year are one in 400 and of dying from cancer one in 600, yet many of us fail to exercise or maintain a healthy diet. We have learned to live with these common threats to our health. Yet we have been afraid to return to the malls and the skies [after the September 11, 2001, terrorist attacks].

Examining the Odds

What are the odds of dying on our next flight or next trip to a shopping mall? There are more than 40,000 malls in this country, and each is open about 75 hours per week. If a person shopped for two hours each week and terrorists were able to destroy one mall per week, the odds of being at the wrong place at the wrong time would be approximately 1.5 million to 1. If terrorists destroyed one mall each month, the odds would climb to one in 6 million. This assumes the total destruction of the entire mall; if that unlikely event didn't occur, the odds would become even more favorable.

In another hypothetical but horrible scenario, let us assume that each week one commercial aircraft was hijacked and crashed. What are the odds that a person who goes on one trip per month would be in that plane? There are currently about 18,000 commercial flights a day, and if that person's trip has four flights associated with it, the odds against that person's being on a crashed plane are about 135,000 to 1. If there were only one hijacked plane per month, the odds would be about 540,000 to 1.

Stories in the news media have begun to consider the virtue of a public relations campaign in Muslim nations to bring our side of the war to the populations of these countries. While this can be an important strategy, I would like to suggest that we need an information campaign in this country as well, because a key element of life after Sept. 11 has not been well presented to the public: Our leaders and media have not done a good job of discussing the risks that citizens need to consider when making choices in their daily lives.

We are presented with a continuous stream of stories telling us about the most recent horrible incident and the possibilities of future terrors. Frequent repetition of these stories may lead people to overestimate the likelihood of future dire events. While we need to be made aware of potential dangers, we also need to understand the true probabilities of these risks. In the above examples, the scenarios were pretty extreme; the odds of any one of us being directly affected by a lesser event would be even more remote.

People tend to underestimate the probability of a common event's occurring but overestimate the probability of a rare event. These findings may be due in part to the frequency with which we are exposed to news stories about the remote versus the common event. Anthrax, which has so far claimed five lives out of a population of 275 million, is a continuous story, while smoking-related illnesses, which claim about 400,000 lives per year, are not a news story at all.

Britt. © 1995 by Copley News Service. Reprinted by permission.

Anthrax is a big story and is worthy of media attention, but people may be overreacting in changing their personal behavior because of this remote event. Perhaps they overestimate the potential probabilities that an anthrax-related incident could happen to them because of the frequency with which they see anthrax-related news stories. In Madison, Wisconsin, it was reported that in some neighborhoods parents didn't allow their children to go trick-or-treating at Halloween because of the heightened risks of terrorism. What are the odds that any single child would be affected by terrorists on that one night?

We need to separate the probability that an event may occur in our country and the probability that it will occur to us as individuals. In making an informed decision about my own behavior, I need to know the probability that I will be personally affected by a terrorist act, not what the probability is that such an act may occur at some place and some time.

We each have many opportunities to take various actions each day. Each opportunity has multiple choices and multiple outcomes. Each of us must independently make our own decisions, but we are being given incomplete information on which to base these decisions. As a result we may have been unnecessarily cautious.

The economic cost to our nation in lost expenditures, resulting in lost jobs and lost businesses, has been enormous. While the impact of any potential event on any one of us is slight, the impact of the sum of our individual behaviors is great. There is a key question that we need to consider: What are the odds that I, myself, will be at the exact wrong place at the exact wrong time?

While any terrorist event is horrible, if I act with respect to my own real risk and the probability that I, personally, will be affected, then I can return to a more normal life. If I act as if each terrorist act will be directed specifically at me, then I will hide, and collectively we will all hide.

> "The sword of [Mohammed] and the
> [Qur'an] are the most stubborn enemies of
> Civilization, Liberty and Truth which the
> world has yet known."

Islam Is a Threat to National Security

Antony Flew

In the following viewpoint, philosopher Antony Flew argues that Islam threatens to destroy Western civilization and create a global Islamic state. According to Flew, Muslims literally interpret and unquestionably accept the prescriptions in the Islamic holy book, the Koran (or Qur'an), which charges Muslims to take over the world. Flew contends that Islam is contemptible of Western ideals—such as democracy, freedom of religion, and toleration—and demands its adherents do whatever is necessary, including using armed force, to overthrow them. Antony Flew is a laureate of the Academy of Humanism in England.

As you read, consider the following questions:

1. Why does Flew believe it is inappropriate to distinguish between moderate and fundamentalist Muslims?
2. What is the expanded definition of *Kufr*, according to the author?
3. According to Sir William Muir, what standard Islamic beliefs continue to flourish?

Antony Flew, "Islam's War Against the West," *Free Inquiry*, vol. 22, Spring 2002, pp. 40–44. Copyright © 2002 by *Free Inquiry*. Reproduced by permission.

I n his letter inviting me to contribute to this issue of *Free Inquiry*, the editor referred to "the thesis expressed by Paul Kurtz, Ibn Warraq, and others "that the [September 11, 2001] terrorist attacks on New York City and Washington, D.C., 'were profoundly religious acts'"; it went on to say that I had 'made predictions about the likelihood of religious terrorism that have proven horribly correct.'" Indeed I had. But why does anyone pretend that these were not profoundly religious acts when Usama bin Laden [the terrorist who masterminded the attacks] himself insists that they were?

With the general public the main reason for this pretense is presumably a nearly if not quite total ignorance of Islamic teachings. But any responsible politician in any of those Christian or post-Christian countries that since World War II have been subjected to substantial immigrations from Muslim countries must, whatever the extent of their knowledge of the teachings of Islam, feel a heavy duty to do all they can to spread the conviction—at least among the members and descendants of those immigrants—that Usama bin Laden's terrorist war against the United States and its allies is radically incompatible with the actual teachings of the Prophet Muhammad.

The True Nature of Islam

But *Free Inquiry* is not a political journal. Our concern here is, therefore, solely with the truth. And the truth is that whereas Christianity, for the first three centuries of its remarkable expansion in the face of successive persecutions, made all its converts by peaceful individual persuasion, Islam already during the later years of the prophet's own lifetime— from the time of the move from Mecca to Medina—was gaining most of its converts in consequence of military victories. And after his death Islam soon showed itself to be—in post-Marxist terms—the uniting and justifying ideology of Arab imperialism. This beginning has had, as we shall see, lasting consequences for the relations between Islam and all other religions.

When in 1920 Bertrand Russell visited the USSR— decades before the Politburo found it convenient to present itself as the protector of the Arabs—he discerned similarities between Bolshevism and Islam: "Bolshevism combines the characteristics of the French Revolution with those of the rise of Islam"; and "Marx has taught that Communism is fatally predestined to come about; this produces a state of mind not unlike that of the early successors of Mahommet." So Russell himself concluded: "Mahommedanism and Bolshevism are practical, social, unspiritual, concerned to win the empire of this world. . . . What Mahommedanism did for the Arabs, Bolshevism may do for the Russians."

As a clear, commendably honest, and altogether authoritative epitome of the totalitarian character of Islam, consider this manifesto issued in Leicester, England, on behalf of the Islamic Council of Europe:

> The religion of Islam embodies the final and most complete word of God. . . . Departmentalisation of life into different watertight compartments, religious and secular, sacred and profane, spiritual and material is ruled out. . . . *Islam is not a religion in the Western understanding of the word. It is a faith and a way of life, a religion and a social order, a doctrine and a code of conduct, a set of values and principles, and a social movement to realise them in history* [emphasis supplied].

In this we have a statement that satisfactorily transcends all differences within and between various Muslim communities, such as those between Sunni and Shi'a, or between the so-called fundamentalists and their opponents. The term *fundamentalist* is anyway in the present case peculiarly inappropriate. It is derived from the title of a series of tracts—*The Fundamentals*—published in the United States in 1909; and it is defined as the belief that the Bible, as the Word of God, is wholly, literally, and infallibly true—a belief that, notoriously, commits fundamentalist Christians to defending the historicity of the accounts of Creation given in the first two chapters of Genesis. To rate as truly a Christian it is by no means necessary to be in this understanding fundamentalist. It is instead fully sufficient to accept the Apostles' and/or the Nicene Creed wholeheartedly. But in order to be properly accounted a Muslim it is essential to be a fundamentalist with regard to (not the Bible but) the Qur'an.

It was his recognition of the truth of those last two heavily emphasized sentences of that statement made on behalf of the Islamic Council of Europe that provoked the conservative prime minister of Italy, Silvio Berlusconi, in the last week of September 2001, boldly to insist that "We must be aware of the superiority of our civilization, a system that has guaranteed the well-being, respect for human rights and—in contrast with Islamic countries—respect for religious and political rights."

Just as soon as they learned that Berlusconi had uttered these words, a bevy of European politicians rushed forward to denounce him. The Belgian prime minister, Guy Verhofstadt, said, "I can hardly believe that the Italian prime minister made such statements." The spokesman for the European Commission, Jean-Christophe Filori, added: "We certainly do not share the views expressed by Signor Berlusconi." Italy's center-left opposition spokesman Giovanni Berlinguer called the words of Berlusconi "eccentric and dangerous." Within days he was effectively forced to withdraw those politically most incorrect words. . . .

Transforming Societies—and the World

It has long been obvious that the same Islamic predispositions—an inability to come to terms with state secularism, religious pluralism, and universal adult suffrage, of which the mirror image is a visceral longing for the hermetic and exclusive theocracy of traditional Islam—have been forming the attitudes of the Muslim immigrant population of Western Europe, especially Britain, in much the same measure as they have those of Muslims elsewhere, confronted with democratic pluralism. A general statement of the Muslim position will be found in Sheikh Shabbir Akhtar's *Be Careful with Muhammad: The Salman Rushdie Affair*. This is far more than just a defense of the Muslim stand in that affair. Despite the author's protestations to the contrary, it is difficult to see it as other than an implicit justification of the Muslims' right to set up an Islamic theocracy in Britain as being what he considers to be the only solution to the problem of the Muslim theocrat's irreconcilable confrontation with secularism. He says:

> Yet one needs to rise above one's ethnocentricity to see what cultural memories the democracy evokes in the Muslim

mind. For theocracy is as precious to Muslims as democracy is to Westerners. . . .

I myself have no difficulty at all in understanding "what cultural memories theocracy evokes in the Muslim mind." But, as usual refusing to heed calls for political correctness, I insist on saying that I have myself no sympathy whatsoever for the egregious arrogance of this demand from recent immigrants and the descendants of recent immigrants into my native land [England]. If they truly find life in a secular state intolerable, why do they not now return to the Islamic states from which they came rather than demanding that the host country make radical constitutional changes to accommodate them?

Quotes from the Qur'an: A Message of War

Let those fight in the cause of God who sell the life of this world for the hereafter. To him who fights in the cause of God, whether he is slain or victorious, soon we shall give him a great reward. (Qur'an, sura 4, verse 74)

Those who believe fight in the cause of God, and those who reject faith fight in the cause of evil. (4:76)

O believers, take not Jews and Christians as friends, they are friends of each other. Those of you who make them his friends is one of them. God does not guide an unjust people. (5:54)

Fight those who believe neither in God nor the Last Day, nor what has been forbidden by God and his messenger [Muhammad], nor acknowledge the religion of Truth [Islam], even if they are People of the Book [Jews and Christians], until they pay the tribute and have been humbled. (9:29)

When you meet the unbelievers, smite their necks, then when you have made wide slaughter among them, tie fast the bonds, then set them free, either by grace or ransom, until the war lays down its burdens. (47:4)

Ibn al-Rawandi, *Free Inquiry*, Spring 2002.

It is characteristic of a secular, pluralist democracy that all religious beliefs are tolerated as long as they remain, within reason, within the limits of personal belief and do not impinge unduly upon those who do not share those beliefs. Or, to put it another way, while religious beliefs are tolerated, religious practices and institutions may not necessarily be accorded the same freedom if they conflict with the law or constitution of the wider state. But this "live and let live" approach is apparently unacceptable to many Muslim spokesmen, of whose attitudes the following quotation is typical: "The implementation of Islam as a complete code of life cannot be limited to the home and to personal relationships. It is to be sought and achieved in society as a whole."

Those words were preached from the *minbar* of Bradford, England's, mosque. A well-known *imam* in France is reported as preaching to the effect that, "There can be no government contrary to what God has revealed" (in the Qur'an). He concludes that it is the duty of every Muslim to overthrow every power "which governs in contravention of that which God enjoins and (to bring about) the erection of the Islamic state." In more moderate terms, but to the same effect, Sheikh Shabbir Ahktar says:

> Our inherited (Islamic) understanding of religious freedom, of the nature and role of religion in society, is in the last analysis being fundamentally challenged by the new religious pluralism in Britain.

Behind this, too, surely lies the plea articulated by [Muhammad Ali] Jinnah [leader of the Muslim League in early twentieth-century India], that Islam must be protected from the consequences of democratic pluralism.

Islam's Hostility Toward the West

Perhaps the most direct expression of Muslim defiance of Western-style democracy is the following, uncompromising statement issued jointly by the two most representative Islamic organizations in Britain, the Islamic Academy of Cambridge, and the Islamic Cultural Centre of London. This statement insists that the Muslim community: "cannot commit itself to follow all 'current laws' however anti-religious these laws may become *through democratic means*" (emphasis supplied).

Quotations are given to illustrate Muslim attitudes of discontent with state neutrality towards Islam: a visceral objection to living under pluralist dispensation: an inability to accept the authority of democratic decision-making when this conflicts with revelation: and a refusal to contemplate the possibility of Islam existing simply as a personal belief system, shorn of its political and social institutions. Such quotations could be multiplied indefinitely. They are clearly constants of the Muslim world outlook whether in the context of post-imperial India, Nigeria, the Sudan, or Muslim settlement in Western Europe.

The nature of this world outlook can be further elucidated by expounding the views of Dr. Kalim Siddiqui, director of the London Muslim Institute. He became locally notorious by publicly calling for Muslims to murder Salman Rushdie, author of *The Satanic Verses*, an indisputably criminal offense for which, since he was an Arab Muslim, he was of course neither arrested nor prosecuted. Siddiqui is the moving spirit of an international Islamic tendency inspired by Ayatollah Khomeini's Iranian Revolution. The aims of this tendency are set out as follows:

> to eliminate all authority other than Allah and His Prophet; to eliminate nationalism in all its shapes and forms, in particular the nation-State; to unite all Islamic movements into a single global Islamic movement to establish the Islamic State; to reestablish a dominant and global Islamic civilisation based on the concept of *Tawheed* [the unity of Allah].

Total Incompatibility

Nationalism, the nation-state, and democracy for Siddiqui represent *Kufr*, literally infidelity but equivalent in a modern context to atheism. Thus the greatest political *Kufr* in the modern world is nationalism, followed closely by democracy ("sovereignty of the people"), socialism ("dictatorship of the proletariat"), capitalism, and free elections. And "modern *kufr* has disguised itself as science, philosophy, technology, democracy and 'progress.'" On the contrary, the "political party framework as found in Western 'democracies' is divisive of the society and therefore does not suit the *Ummah*" (the worldwide Islamic community). He concludes that "one *Ummah* must mean one Islamic movement, leading to one global Islamic State under one Imam/Khalifa [Caliph]."

For Siddiqui, "there is no compatibility whatsoever between Islam and the west" and the Islamic Movement "regards the west as totally incompatible with Islam." The notion that a Muslim may live under the government of non-Islamic nation-state and still practice his Islam as a personal belief system is apparently unacceptable to Siddiqui, for "A Muslim can neither live the 'good life' on his own nor pursue 'personal *taqwa*' [faithfulness to Allah] in isolation." Dr. Siddiqui concluded one of his published essays with the following rallying cry, addressed to his fellow Muslims among whom, one must assume, are those in Britain:

> Just as the power and influence of *kufr* in the modern world is global, so are the bonds of faith and destiny of the Muslim *Immah*. History has come full circle. The global power of *kufr* waits to be challenged and defeated by the global power of Islam. This is the unfinished business of history, so let us go ahead and finish it.

The achievement of Siddiqui's aims certainly does not exclude armed force: "Lightly-armed *muttawi* [faithful to Allah] soldiers who go out to fight and die for Islam are more powerful than the heavily-armed professional soldiers who fear death."

Moreover, the odds are in Islam's favor: "With a population of almost one billion and with infinite sources of wealth, you can defeat all the powers." It is therefore possible for the Muslims to bring about "the total transformation of the world."

Dr. Siddiqui is particularly scornful of the compromisers who have been trying to prove Islam compatible with their secular ambitions and Western preferences, and contemptuous of those who seek to set up "a liberal and democratic nation-State with a few cosmetic 'Islamic' features."

Resistance to Reform

The moral from all that British material is absolutely clear. If we are to understand the nature of Islam, and to meet and overcome the threat that it presents to the entire Western world, we have now to abandon assumptions that were sufficiently realistic when we were dealing with earlier threats to that world. Before World War II, for instance, it was common to speak of the United States as a tri-faith country. During that war a popular song insisted that the "Smiths and the Jones, the Kellys and Cohns" were all equally committed to the war effort of the U.S.A. That was their country as Americans, regardless of their present religious beliefs or the countries from which their parents or grandparents had originated. After that war, President [Dwight] Eisenhower made a remark that my theologian father thought could only have been made by an American president: "Everyone must have a religion, and I don't care what it is." Such indifference was all very well, indeed properly presidential, at a time when the United States had no significant number of Muslim citizens.

Certainly it is possible for people professedly committed to aggressively incompatible religious beliefs to live together in friendly toleration. But this is achieved only by the more or less conscious and explicit abandonment of those of their pretended beliefs that would make such friendly and tolerant cohabitation impossible. So the possibility of such cohabitation is irrelevant to the question of what the relevant teachings of the Qur'an actually are. But because of these possibilities of friendly cohabitation it was not preposterous for President Bill Clinton to say in 1994, *in an address to the Jordanian Parliament:*

> After all, the chance to live in harmony with our neighbors and to build a better life for our children is the hope that binds us all together. Whether we worship in a mosque in Irbid, a Baptist church like my own in Little Rock, Arkansas, or a synagogue in Haifa, we are bound together by that hope.

It was not preposterous for President Clinton to say this in an address to the parliament of a country of which almost the entire population is Muslim. For Jordan—unlike, for instance, Iraq and Saudi Arabia—does have an effective parliament, and its king at that time was a man who had made peace with Israel and succeeded in defeating a terrorist offensive against his own country. But for an account of the actual teachings of the Qur'an and of their great and growing threat to Western civilization it will be instructive to attend to a warning from an earlier century.

Sir William Muir's *Life of Mahomet*, based on original Muslim sources, appeared in Edinburgh in four volumes between 1856 and 1861. Muir's judgement on the life, which was to be repeated over and over again by subsequent scholars, was based upon a distinction between its earlier Meccan and later Medinan period. In Mecca, Muhammad was a sincere, religiously motivated seeker after truth. In Medina, Muhammad the man showed his feet of clay, and was corrupted by power and by worldly ambitions.

Muir went on to say that so long as the Qur'an remained the standard of Islamic belief certain evils would continue to flourish: "Polygamy, divorce and slavery strike at the root of public morals, poison domestic life, and disorganize society; while the Veil removes the female sex from its just position and influence in the world. . . . Freedom of thought and private judgement are crushed and annihilated. Toleration is unknown, and the possibility of free and liberal institutions is foreclosed." Muir's final judgement was: "The sword of Mahomet and the Coran [the Qur'an] are the most stubborn enemies of Civilization, Liberty and Truth which the world has yet known."

"Islam—as a religion, culture and society—most emphatically is not an enemy of the West."

Islam Is Not a Threat to National Security

Antony T. Sullivan

According to Antony T. Sullivan in the following viewpoint, contrary to claims by some prominent scholars, Islam does not pose a threat to the security of Western nations. On the contrary, he asserts, Islam is a religion of compassion and mercy, and most followers of Islam condemn terrorist attacks like the one that occurred on September 11, 2001. Sullivan insists that setting up Islam as an enemy of the West could result in a war of civilizations that the United States will not win. Sullivan, a senior scholar of the Center for Middle Eastern and North African Studies at the University of Michigan, has written several books and articles about Islam.

As you read, consider the following questions:

1. What are the three Abrahamic faiths, according to Sullivan?
2. As cited by the author, to what extent does the Koran endorse war?
3. Why is the Muslim world angry with Americans and other Westerners, in Sullivan's view?

Islam—as a religion, culture and society—most emphatically is not an enemy of the West.

Those who argue the contrary slander not only the third and last of the three great Abrahamic revelations but make all too likely the outbreak of either a religious war pitting Christianity (and perhaps Judaism) against Islam or a war of civilizations pitting the West against the entire Muslim world. And be assured: Any wars of religion or civilization will not be wars that the West—or the United States—will win.

This, of course, does not mean that the war now under way should not be prosecuted in the most energetic, merciless and sustained fashion possible. But to the extent feasible it should be fought as a *guerre de l'ombre* (a war in the shadows), focusing on destruction of the Afghani sources of international terrorism and the overthrow of the Taliban regime. Unless incontrovertible evidence is adduced of involvement of any state other than Afghanistan in [the September 11, 2001, terrorist attacks,] public bombing or ground campaigns should be limited to Afghanistan alone. Under no circumstances should the war be permitted to degenerate into any "war of civilizations" or to be perceived by Arabs or Muslims as such.

A Clash of Civilizations?

Years before the attack on the World Trade Center and the Pentagon, distinguished scholars such as professors Samuel Huntington of Harvard University and Bernard Lewis of Princeton University, and publicists such as Daniel Pipes and Steven Emerson, were suggesting the possibility of clashes between Islam and the West, and the likelihood that Muslims worldwide might support terrorism to destroy Western civilization. Their work, implicitly or explicitly, prepared the ground for the U.S. Anti-Terrorism Act of 1996 and the consequent jailings without charge of up to 19 Arabs or Muslims in the United States. At least one of the individuals imprisoned was held for more than three years. No evidence of culpability of any of these individuals ever was adduced publicly, and most of these Arab or Muslim detainees are fortunately now free on court order. Ideas—particularly those of distinguished scholars—do have consequences, and bad ideas may indeed have very bad consequences.

Judaism, Christianity and Islam all trace their origins back at least to the Old Testament prophet Abraham. Each of these three religions venerates him. Each of these Abrahamic faiths has similarities with the other two, and each historically has produced civilizations and societies with recognizably similar characteristics.

Not only is Islam not an enemy of the West, but it, like Judaism, is part of the larger civilizational ecumene that we in the contemporary West know—or ought to. In fact, the West stops at the Indus, not at the Dardanelles. Today, Islam is part and parcel of the West, just as the West is part and parcel of Islam.

A Religion of Compassion and Mercy

What occurred on Sept. 11 was first and foremost an attack on Islam itself. Specifically, that criminal operation constituted an attack on the values of compassion, beneficence and mercy that pervade the Koran and that historically have characterized the practice of Islam. The ignorant terrorists responsible for the operation of Sept. 11 might have done well to reread the *fatiha* (the eight opening lines) of the Koran. There, they would have found compassion and mercy mentioned a total of four times.

And they would have done well to read Chapter 5, Verse 32 of the Koran: "We prescribed . . . that whosoever kills a person, unless it be for manslaughter or for mischief in the land, it is as though he had killed all mankind. And whosoever saves a life, it is as though he had saved the lives of all men."

Moreover, had they consulted additional portions of the Koran, they might have discovered that the planned operation only could have been undertaken by Muslim apostates. To the extent that the Koran endorses war at all, it endorses only defensive combat designed to protect the Islamic community in the most dire of circumstances. No faithful Muslim possibly could justify the operation of Sept. 11 within that limitation.

The Koran includes passages invoking violence. But so does the Old Testament, in considerable number. To wit, Deuteronomy 32:42: "I will make my arrows drunk with blood, and my sword shall devour flesh; and that with the blood of the slain and of the captives, from the long-haired heads of the enemy." (See also Deuteronomy 2:34, 3:6 and 7:2.) Evocations of violence in religious texts is one of many elements the Abrahamic religions share.

Quotes from the Koran: A Message of Peace

"God loves those who judge equitably." (5:42)

"God loves the patient." (3:145)

"And one of His signs is the creation of the heaven and earth and the diversity of your languages and colours; surely there are signs in this for the learned." (30:22)

"Even if you stretch out your hand against me to kill me, I shall not stretch Out my hand against you to kill you. I fear Allah, the Lord of the World." (5:28)

"Whosoever does a good deed, male or female—those shall enter paradise, therein provided without reckoning." (40:40)

"Take to forgiveness and enjoin good and turn aside from the ignorant." (7:199)

New Internationalist, May 2002.

Contemporary terrorists who invoke Islam to justify their actions are utterly ignorant of classical Islamic law. Muslim jurisprudence is categorical: It prescribes the harshest penalties, including death, for terrorism. Crimes defined as terroristic and/or criminal in classical jurisprudence include the poisoning of wells, abduction, brigandage, night assaults and rape. Modern terrorists who proclaim themselves Muslims seem unaware that the Koran makes clear that the injustice of others in no way excuses any injustice of one's own.

Most Muslims Condemn Terrorism

For almost a decade Muslim religious leaders and public figures have been sponsoring international conferences designed to demonstrate the fallacy of any notion of Islam being an enemy of the West or the likelihood of any clash of civilizations. I know, because I have participated in several of these conferences. Those who persist in merchandising notions of Islam being an enemy of the West should know that there is an almost universal rejection of this idea in the Muslim world itself. Such writers mislead Western public opinion and alienate Muslims everywhere who otherwise might be only too glad to be friends with the West.

The Sept. 11 attack has been publicly and categorically condemned by the most important Islamist leaders and public figures in the world. On Sept. 24 the London-based Arabic daily *al Quds al Arabi* published a statement in which more than 75 such individuals forcefully denounced the "terrorist aggression on large American installations which killed innocent victims belonging to more than 60 countries." They described the tragedy as a "crime against humanity" and called upon all believers in the sanctity of human life to "denounce and fight against terrorism wherever it is and regardless of the ethnicity or religion of those involved in it." These Islamists added that "all those proved to have committed terrorist acts against humanity . . . should be tried and punished, without any kind of allowances."

Rather than any antipathy emanating from Islam, Americans and other Westerners should recognize that anger toward the United States in the Muslim world emanates primarily from the rage at specific American policies. U.S. partiality to Israel at the expense of Palestinians, maintenance of sanctions on Iraq that fail to weaken [Iraqi leader] Saddam Hussein while resulting in the death of half-a-million Iraqi children, and consistent failure to support individual liberty and limited government in Muslim states are among their major grievances. Those who pontificate on Islam somehow being an enemy of the West almost never mention or grant any legitimacy to this list of complaints. And these grievances are fully shared by the 7 million American citizens who now are Muslim.

The Circle of Tradition and Progress

One of the most promising contemporary initiatives in interfaith and intercivilizational dialogue is the Circle of Tradition and Progress, which brings together distinguished Western and Muslim (Islamist) thinkers to explore and combat the worldwide challenge of radical secular modernity. The philosophic basis for this joint enterprise is the thought (from the Western tradition) of such thinkers as Thomas Aquinas, Edmund Burke, Eric Voegelin, Gerhart Niemeyer and Russell Kirk. Muslim participants adduce Islamic thinkers of similar philosophic orientations. In distinction to speculations about impending civilizational conflict, the Circle of Tradition and Progress represents a practical ecumenical endeavor whereby the West and the Islamic world may jointly address the viruses of modernity that today so threaten us all.

The statement of purpose of the Circle of Tradition and Progress offers sage advice on how to conduct international relations. The statement reads: "We favor the conduct of international relations on a basis of respect for all of the world's civilizations. We oppose all attempts to export or impose cultural systems, to support dictatorial regimes or to obstruct democratic transformation. It is our conviction that attempts to reinvent the Cold War with Muslims targeted as enemies of the West, or the West as enemies of Islam, are deplorable and should be avoided. We are united in our belief that all such Manichaean formulations will impede cooperation between Muslims and the West, and are likely over time to have a dramatically negative impact on both international stability and world peace." Bush-administration officials charged with responding to the Sept. 11 attack might well be guided by such counsel.

If the contemporary tendency to depict Islam as an enemy of the West is unconscionable, it also is understandable. So is the popular receptivity to this perverse idea that characterizes Western culture.

The roots of this disposition reach back at least as far as the Crusades. The Western conviction of an alien and menacing Islamic "other" was solidified by the centuries of war between the Ottoman Empire and Western and Central Europe. It was exacerbated by European colonialism and the Christian missionary enterprise of the 19th century and the evangelical revival today, and it currently flourishes as a result of the serious challenge that the Islamic revival presents to the long-term viability of the state of Israel.

It is not by chance that those most frequently proclaiming that Islam is an enemy of the West are themselves fervent partisans of Israel or (as in the case of former Israeli prime minister Benjamin Netanyahu), Israelis themselves. Islam is in no way a challenge to the West, but in its political form it may well present a threat to Israel. If so, that is Israel's problem, not ours. Israel alone can mitigate any Islamic threat only by dealing justly with all its neighbors, and most specifically with the Palestinians.

As a Republican and a conservative, I call on my philosophical comrades in arms to reject the anti-Islamic triumphalist warmongering of neoconservative ideologues. And I urge all Americans to repudiate any belief that Islam is an enemy of the West. This idea is wrong. Worse, it is dangerous. To all of us. Especially now.

"The consequences of an attack with smallpox are potentially catastrophic."

Biological Weapons Threaten National Security

Veronique de Rugy and Charles V. Peña

In the following viewpoint Veronique de Rugy and Charles V. Peña argue that biological weapons present a greater threat to America's security than either nuclear or chemical weapons. The authors contend that unlike nuclear and chemical attacks, an assault using biological weapons would not be detected immediately, giving the virus time to spread throughout the population before any antidote could be administered. According to de Rugy and Peña, smallpox is an especially serious threat because of its high fatality rate and ease of transmission. Veronique de Rugy is a policy analyst and Charles V. Peña is a senior defense policy analyst at the Cato Institute, a libertarian public policy research foundation.

As you read, consider the following questions:
1. How many Americans were killed by the 1918 influenza epidemic, according to de Rugy and Peña?
2. According to the authors, what was the Dark Winter exercise?
3. How many died seven weeks into the Dark Winter exercise, as related by the authors?

Veronique de Rugy and Charles V. Peña, "Responding to the Threat of Smallpox Terrorism," *Policy Analysis*, April 18, 2002, pp. 2–4, 13. Copyright © 2002 by The Cato Institute. Reproduced by permission.

In the wake of [the September 11, 2001, terrorist attacks], the potential use of weapons of mass destruction (WMD) by terrorists cannot be dismissed or ignored. Osama bin Laden has claimed that his al-Qaeda terrorist organization [deemed responsible for the September 11 attacks] has nuclear and chemical weapons and is not afraid to use them. Such statements might be considered more boastful bluff and bluster than real threats, but there should be no doubting bin Laden's desire for WMD. In May 1998 he issued a statement titled "The Nuclear Bomb of Islam," which stated that "it is the duty of Muslims to prepare as much force as possible to terrorize the enemies of God." In an interview with *Time* magazine in December 1998, bin Laden said, "If I have indeed acquired these weapons, then I thank God for enabling me to do so."

There is evidence that al-Qaeda members have been trying to acquire nuclear materials since at least 1994 and have experimented with using chemical weapons (cyanide). Intelligence sources have pointed to an al-Qaeda training camp (called abu-Khabab after the Egyptian chemical-biological weapons expert who directed it) outside Jalalabad, Afghanistan, as a chemical and biological weapons training facility. And a manual ("Encyclopedia of Afghan Resistance") distributed on CD-ROM includes a section on how to make chemical and biological weapons. Finally, there is evidence that the September 11 terrorists were interested in crop-dusters, which could be used to distribute a chemical or biological agent.

Terrorism and WMD

Although the use of any WMD by a terrorist group would be an event of devastating proportions, there are differences worth noting and understanding between potential nuclear, chemical, and biological terrorist attacks. A low-yield nuclear weapon would cause immediate damage to a circumscribed area by explosive blast, overpressure, extreme heat, and radiation. If such a weapon were detonated in a major metropolitan area, the casualties would likely be in excess of 100,000 dead, injured, and subjected to lethal doses of radiation.

The Aum Shinrikyo cult used a chemical weapon, Sarin (a nerve agent so deadly that a single drop on the skin can be fatal) in the 1995 Tokyo subway attack. The attack was not a complete success because of ineffective dissemination, but 12 people died and nearly 3,800 were injured. Aum Shinrikyo also used VX (10 to 1,000 times stronger than Sarin) in four other attacks. Those attacks were targeted against specific individuals or groups of people rather than aimed at inflicting massive casualties. In one instance, there was 1 fatality and in another 20 deaths, but the other attacks failed because of ineffective release of the VX agent. It is estimated that, under ideal conditions, a quart of VX properly distributed in a major metropolitan area could kill about 12 million people in 60 minutes.

As catastrophic as either a nuclear or a chemical terrorist attack would be, the effects of the attack would be immediate and limited to people in the vicinity of the attack. Although the damage and casualties would likely be an order of magnitude or more greater than those of the World Trade Center attacks, it would be possible to know that an attack had taken place and respond accordingly. According to D.A. Henderson at Johns Hopkins University, "After an explosion or a chemical attack, the worst effects are quickly over, the dimensions of the catastrophe can be defined, the toll of injuries and deaths can be ascertained, and efforts can be directed to stabilization and recovery."

Bioterrorism Is Different from Nuclear or Chemical Attacks

The nature of bioterrorism, however, is very different from that of nuclear or chemical attacks. Biological agents are disease-causing organisms. If the organisms used are contagious pathogens, their effects can be passed on unknowingly, thereby spreading the damage well beyond the people who are initially infected. If successful, a smallpox attack could be more devastating than even a nuclear weapon. Unlike a nuclear or chemical attack, a biological attack would not be detected immediately; there is usually an incubation period of several days to a few weeks before the first symptoms appear in infected persons. Furthermore, it would be difficult to know immediately whether infection was the result of a *natural outbreak* of a disease or of a premeditated release of the pathogen. And even if there is an antidote for the disease, detection of the attack

The "A" List

The biggest biological threats, according to the Centers for Disease Control:

- *Anthrax:* Starts with flulike symptoms; lethal without antibiotics
- *Smallpox:* Starts with fever, aches, vomiting; progresses to body blisters; often fatal
- *Pneumonic plague:* Symptoms include fever, chills and cough; without early treatment, causes breathing trouble and death
- *Botulinum toxin:* This toxin, often the culprit in food poisoning, can cause blurry vision, then whole-body paralysis that can last for months
- *Tularemia:* Inhaling this bacteria can cause fever and a pneumonialike illness; rarely fatal, particularly when treated with antibiotics
- *Filoviruses:* Ebola and other filoviruses cause fever and internal bleeding; rapidly fatal and no treatment is available
- *Arenaviruses:* Lassa fever and other arenaviruses cause symptoms that include fever and vomiting; usually not fatal with treatment

Laura Johannes and Marilyn Chase, *Wall Street Journal*, September 28, 2001.

may occur too late for the antidote to be effective.

The devastation that could be caused by a biological attack can be demonstrated by the natural outbreak of influenza in the United States during the winter of 1918–19. The first signs of the influenza virus (the symptoms being no different than those of a common cold, which further highlights the difficulties associated with detecting and diagnosing biological infection) occurred in the spring of 1918 in military camps throughout the United States. American soldiers carried the flu to Europe where it mutated into a killer virus. Returning troops brought the disease back to the United States where it spread to the civilian population. By the fall of 1918 the United States was in the grips of an influenza epidemic that killed an estimated 675,000 Americans. But, unlike a natural outbreak of a disease such as influenza, a bioterrorist attack would be an intentional release of a deadly disease by a thinking enemy intent on inflicting mass casualties. In all likelihood, an effective bioterrorist attack would ultimately exact a similar or greater toll.

The threat of bioterrorism is especially worrisome because of the vulnerability of the U.S. population to such an attack. Indeed, according to the Chemical and Biological Arms Control Institute, "The vulnerabilities of the United States to bioterrorism attack are virtually infinite." As a result, the problem of bioterrorism can paralyze policymakers and response planners. Frequently, such a large threat is downplayed, dismissed, or ignored. For example, Milton Leitenberg at the Center for International and Security Studies at the University of Maryland wrote (before September 11), "As regards bioterrorism, the current national discussion is characterized by gross exaggeration, hype, and abstract vulnerability assessments." Leitenberg further asserted, "The greatest problem that the United States—and the world—face regarding biological weapons is their proliferation among nation states, and *not the potential of their use by non-state, or 'terrorist' actors.*" In other words—at least before September 11—Leitenberg thought not only that the threat of bioterrorism was exaggerated but also that terrorists were not the problem the United States should focus on. September 11 demonstrated that the United States can ill afford such an attitude.

No one can predict a bioterrorist attack with high certainty and confidence. But a simple "back of the envelope" threat assessment using a model used by Colonel Lani Kass (USAF, Retired) at the National War College,

$$\text{Vulnerability} \times \text{Intentions} \times \text{Capabilities} = \text{Threat}$$

provides insight about and understanding of the potential of a future bioterrorist attack. The vulnerability of the United States to such an attack is quite high. The attacks on the World Trade Center and the Pentagon demonstrate the seriousness of al-Qaeda's intentions. The big unknown is whether al-Qaeda possesses the capabilities to carry out an attack with biological weapons. But, as demonstrated by September 11, the United States can ill afford to ignore the possibility.

The Smallpox Threat

A bioterrorist attack could come in one (or more) of many forms (plague, smallpox, or anthrax, for example). Of those, smallpox is the threat most often discussed. Concerns about smallpox as a potential bioweapon were heightened when Ken Alibek, a former deputy director of the Soviet Union's civilian bioweapons program, alleged that the Soviet government produced the smallpox virus in large quantities and weaponized it. Alibek also contended that Russia continued the program after the disintegration of the USSR. Given the deterioration of the Russian military and the supporting industrial complex, there are legitimate concerns that equipment, expertise, and possibly even the virus or weaponized smallpox could have fallen into non-Russian hands.

Smallpox is an especially serious threat because of its high case-fatality rate (30 percent or more of unvaccinated persons) and transmissibility (it spreads easily via inhalation of droplets or direct contact with contaminated objects such as clothing or bed linens). There is also no known effective treatment for smallpox. Smallpox has long been feared as the most devastating of all infectious diseases (before its supposed eradication from the world in 1978, smallpox had killed more people than any other infectious disease in human history), and its potential for devastation is far greater today since there has been no routine vaccination in the United States for more than 25 years. Therefore, in a highly susceptible and mobile population, smallpox would be able to spread widely and rapidly.

The smallpox virus is also easy to disperse. It is one of the smallest living organisms and can be easily prepared as an aerosol and released into the air in a crowded place such as a shopping mall or a sports stadium. Or a suicide terrorist with the virus could infect passersby simply by coughing and sneezing, which can release millions of virus particles into the air.

One example of the magnitude of the consequences of a potential bioterrorist attack with smallpox is the Dark Winter exercise conducted in June 2001. Dark Winter was a fictional scenario depicting a terrorist attack using smallpox released via aerosol at three shopping malls in Oklahoma, Georgia, and Pennsylvania. On day 1 of the crisis (nine days after initial exposure), all that was known was that some two dozen people reported to hospitals in Oklahoma City (there were no similar signs of potential outbreak in Georgia and

Pennsylvania where the dispersion was not as effective but nonetheless resulted in infected people) with flulike symptoms of a strange illness, which was later confirmed by the Centers for Disease Control as smallpox. Assuming that each case was expected to infect at least 10 other people, on day 6 of the crisis there were 2,000 known cases of smallpox and 300 deaths. Due to limited amounts (12 million doses) on hand, the reserve of smallpox vaccine was effectively used up on day 6. By day 12 of the crisis, there were 3,000 cases and 1,000 dead in 25 states. With no vaccine, the smallpox virus was projected to explode as follows:

- After 3 weeks: 30,000 cases and 10,000 dead
- After 5 weeks: 300,000 cases and 100,000 dead
- After 7 weeks: 3 million cases and 1 million dead

It is important to emphasize that the purpose of the Dark Winter exercise was not to make the case that smallpox is the weapon most likely to be used in a bioterrorist attack (it is impossible to make such predictions). However, the Dark Winter exercise did demonstrate that the use of a contagious pathogen as a weapon of bioterrorism can have devastating and far-reaching effects. The consequences of an attack with smallpox are potentially catastrophic, and such an attack is the only external threat to the continued existence of the United States other than a massive nuclear attack from Russia. Therefore, even if likelihood cannot be established, the effects of smallpox as a weapon of bioterrorism warrant taking the threat seriously in order to understand the efficacy of potential response options. Also, preventive measures, which might act as a potential deterrent, reduce the risk, and mitigate the consequences of an attack, need to be examined and evaluated. . . .

A Serious Threat That Deserves Attention

Judging from the September 11 attacks, the threat of direct terrorist attack against the United States is real. And the subsequent anthrax cases point to the possibility of a future bioterrorist attack, possibly using the deadly smallpox virus. The nature of terrorism is such that it is impossible to accurately predict the probability of such an attack, but the potential consequences are catastrophic. Therefore, it is a serious threat that deserves serious attention.

"The history of germ warfare suggests that its combat potential is very limited against a modern society."

The Threat Posed by Biological Weapons Has Been Exaggerated

Steve Bonta

Steve Bonta maintains in the following viewpoint that the risk posed by germ warfare has been exaggerated by those interested in implementing draconion state and federal policies designed to contain a possible outbreak of smallpox or anthrax. He contends that although biological warfare was used successfully in earlier centuries, such an attack would fail against a modern society with good sanitation and advanced medicine. Bonta points to the anthrax attacks in the fall of 2001—which infected only a handful of people—as a demonstration of the limitations of germ warfare. Bonta is a contributing editor for the *New American*, a conservative weekly newsmagazine.

As you read, consider the following questions:
1. What did the original draft of the MEHPA authorize, as reported by Bonta?
2. According to the author, what caused the Black Death?
3. Why would terrorists never engineer a "superflu," in Bonta's opinion?

Steve Bonta, "Prescription for Tyranny," *The New American*, vol. 18, March 25, 2002, pp. 37–39. Copyright © 2002 by *The New American*. Reproduced by permission.

A dangerous new epidemic is incubating in Washington and in state legislatures nationwide, courtesy of the war on terrorism. No, it isn't anthrax or smallpox or bubonic plague or some other deadly germ brewed by bioterrorists. It's a new push, instigated by the Centers for Disease Control (CDC), to toughen state "emergency health powers" laws to enable governors, in conjunction with federal authorities, to exercise police-state powers in the event of another episode of bioterrorism, or even a natural epidemic.

Against the backdrop of [the September 11, 2001, terrorist attacks'] eye-searing drama, the subsequent anthrax attacks on Capitol Hill and the major news media seemed inconspicuous, considering their low infection rate and even lower death toll. Yet with federal authorities now pushing aggressively for new state-level enforcement powers—including draconian powers to round up, quarantine, and forcibly test and vaccinate citizens in the event of an outbreak of smallpox or some other dangerous disease—the anthrax episode may yet profoundly affect the American political landscape.

From Disease Control to People Control

On October 30, 2001, the CDC released the Model State Emergency Health Powers Act (MEHPA) and disseminated copies of the act to legislators in all 50 states. At the time, Secretary of Health and Human Services Tommy Thompson praised the model legislation as "an important tool for state and local officials to respond to bioterrorism and other public health emergencies." But the MEHPA soon attracted attention from critics, and for good reason: Prepared by the Center for Law and the Public's Health at Georgetown and Johns Hopkins Universities, the model legislation was an undisguised recipe for state-level tyranny.[1]

The original draft of the MEHPA authorizes governors to declare states of emergency, which legislatures may not challenge for 60 days. During such a period, according to the terms of Article IV (subtitled "Control of Property"), the state may confiscate any private property, "includ[ing] but not lim-

---

1. The MEHPA bill was signed by President George W. Bush in 2001.

ited to, communication devices, carriers, real estate, fuels, food, clothing, and health care facilities." Additionally, the state is given blanket authority to ration, control, or prohibit the sale or use of "food, fuel, clothing and other commodities, alcoholic beverages, firearms, explosives, and combustibles."

Nor is that the worst of it. Article V, subtitled "Control of Persons," would grant state governments the emergency power "to compel a person to submit to a physical examination and or testing," to "require any physician or other health care provider to perform the medical examination," and to forcibly quarantine any individuals deemed potential disease carriers or refusing to submit to tests. The proposed legislation makes a feeble concession to "due process," requiring a court order to quarantine any individual, but then nullifies the provision by permitting health authorities to quarantine without a court order any time that "delay in the isolation or quarantine of the person would pose an immediate threat to the public health."

After the model law drew negative attention, the CDC came out with a revised version in late December, a kinder, gentler program that delicately struck out overt references to firearms confiscation and changed "control of persons" to "protection of persons"—while keeping intact vague language from which unlimited police powers can still be inferred.

Alarmingly, the MEHPA is already popping up in state legislatures across the country, generally reproduced verbatim from the CDC original, except for cosmetic references to state law and facilities. For example, the legislatures of Pennsylvania, New York, and Illinois are all considering "Emergency Health Powers" acts, faithful reproductions of the October 30th original, complete with references to firearms controls and "control" of persons. Many other states, including Tennessee, Nebraska, Delaware, and California, have introduced "Emergency Health Powers" acts identical to the December draft of the MEHPA, or are designing their own legislation to conform to MEHPA standards.

Capitalizing on the "Alarm of the Day"

Another document published by the CDC, "Isolation and Quarantine Guidelines," makes the beltway perspective on bioterrorism and epidemics crystal clear: The domestic threat of a serious epidemic, unleashed either by bioterrorists or by natural causes, is ample justification for federal oversight and interference with state autonomy, not to mention the occasional exercise of police-state powers under the guise of "states of emergency." Focusing on the *alarum du jour*—the alleged danger of a new terrorist-concocted smallpox epidemic—the CDC document declares that "each state must undertake a review of their own authorities and revise and update their laws to assure sufficient legal powers to carry out an effective response." The document enthusiastically recommends the MEHPA, which "would give state officials broad powers to close buildings, take over hospitals and order quarantines during a biological attack." As for limits on federal power to intervene, "while the Constitution reserves the police power to the States, the Federal government has extensive authority over public health by virtue of the Commerce Clause of the U.S. Constitution, which grants the Federal government the exclusive power to regulate interstate and foreign commerce." This is arrant nonsense; only a federal agency could define a spreading, life-threatening epidemic as a form of "commerce"!

The Stuff of Science Fiction

Although bacteria and other microorganisms can sicken or even kill an individual, their ability to spread and cause "secondary" cases is limited. There is a sound biological reason that the threat of an epidemic from a lethal "Andromeda strain" [anthrax] is largely the stuff of science fiction: Bacteria and viruses need living hosts to provide shelter and sustenance if they are to survive, and therefore they cannot kill those hosts too quickly and too often.

Henry I. Miller, *San Diego Union-Tribune*, September 28, 2000.

In yielding to federal demands to conform with national guidelines and standards, the real danger behind the MEHPA drive is precisely that the states are ceding power and precedent for further federal encroachment to hysteria-mongers in Washington, who view state autonomy with narrow suspicion and seize upon any national emergency, real or feigned, to attack state sovereignty.

States and local governments have occasionally exercised extraordinary powers of seizure, medication, and quarantine, with varying degrees of effectiveness. The state of Minnesota, for example, quarantined lumbermen ill with smallpox and prevented them from leaving their camps during various smallpox epidemics in the late 19th and early 20th centuries. By and large, though, quarantines and mass vaccinations were carried out locally and on a voluntary basis, and often were very successful. In 1947, responding to a smallpox outbreak in New York City, more than six million people voluntarily received vaccinations within a few weeks at stations set up all around the city. While city officials requested help from the military and the U.S. Public Health Service, there were no forced quarantines or mandatory examinations and treatment. Instead, thanks to a massive public information campaign, coupled with the natural desire of sensible people to protect life and limb against a deadly disease, a potential epidemic was contained to nine cases in New York and seven deaths.

In stark contrast, consider the response in [Marshall] Tito's Communist Yugoslavia to a smallpox outbreak in 1972. After a Muslim pilgrim came home from Mecca with smallpox, the disease spread rapidly, infecting patients and staff at the local hospital where he first sought medical attention, then dozens more at a second hospital in Belgrade where he was transferred. The disease ultimately spread to almost 200 others, whereupon Tito—after much of the damage had already been done, it is important to note—declared martial law, prohibited unauthorized travel, seized hotels and apartment houses, and cordoned off entire city blocks with barbed wire and police guards. Millions of Yugoslavs were forcibly vaccinated, and after two months the epidemic was finally brought under control. That our own leaders are now promoting emergency health powers that mirror those practiced in Communist Yugoslavia should give pause for thought.

The Black Death

But what of the modern risk of bioterrorism and germ warfare, and the possible reappearance of a disease like smallpox, against which most modern-day Americans have not been adequately vaccinated? Surely the risk of an artificial epidemic launched by some shadowy terrorist cell or hostile regime is novel and severe enough to justify extraordinary new federal powers!

In the first place, not only is germ warfare not new, it has become less of a threat with advances in medical technology. Consider that the worst catastrophe in Western history in the last thousand years, in terms of human mortality—the bubonic plague pandemic in Europe, also known as the "Black Death"—probably resulted from germ warfare. The plague was brought to Italy in 1847 in the ships of Genovese merchants fleeing from the Black Sea trading port of Kaffa, where besieging Tartar armies, unable to breach the formidable defenses of that city, had catapulted the plague-ridden corpses of certain of their comrades over the walls. The panicked Genovese fled in their boats, and by the time their ships reached port, all aboard were dead or dying. The plague jumped ship and raced across Europe, killing an estimated 25 million people, or up to one-third of the entire population. So great was the trauma of this disaster that kingdoms fell, societies and mores disintegrated, and entire districts were left desolate of human inhabitants. In terms of human toll, the world has never seen another act of warfare even remotely comparable to the Black Death.

Over the ensuing centuries, the tactic of casting germ-ridden corpses and offal over city walls to end sieges was used quite effectively, because of the crowded, unsanitary conditions in medieval cities and the lack of knowledge about the cause of diseases and the way they spread. In more modern times, the British used germ warfare in the French and Indian war, with devastating results: Suspecting that certain Indian tribes were secretly in cahoots with the French, they gifted to the Indians blankets contaminated with small-pox, leading to epidemics that killed hundreds of Indians and virtually wiped out entire tribes.

Back to the Present

However, germ warfare has been far less effective in recent years because of advances in medical technology and epidemiology. The causes of bubonic plague and how it spreads are now clearly understood. Diagnosed in time, it is now a treatable if still dangerous disease, and the unsanitary conditions that once allowed it to wreak havoc—human contact with rats and the fleas they carry—have been largely eradicated from the modern world. Smallpox has been almost completely eradicated as well, except for a few cultures kept under tight security in government laboratories. And even if bioterrorists or a hostile government contrived to unleash smallpox, the disease is generally not contagious until the telltale pustules appear and the victim is generally hospitalized, a factor that severely limits its potential to create a large-scale epidemic. Tropical haemorrhagic fevers like the dreaded Ebola virus are unlikely to survive outside of the equatorial tropics. And, as everyone now realizes, anthrax is not ordinarily a contagious disease. It may be spread in other ways, like the postal service or airborne aerosols, but an outbreak of anthrax hardly merits mass quarantining and police-state powers.

The worst epidemic the United States has ever experienced was the great Spanish Flu epidemic of 1918, and it is unlikely that any bioterrorists would be able to engineer a "superflu" in any event. Besides, using a pathogen as contagious as influenza for any kind of germ warfare would be counterproductive, since it could not be contained by any means and would likely sweep the globe, attacking the target nation and aggressor alike.

[The] anthrax outbreaks [during the fall of 2001] demonstrated the reality of bioterrorism and its limitations. The history of germ warfare suggests that its combat potential is very limited against a modern society living in sanitary conditions and equipped with the best modern medicine. And the comparative histories of the authoritarian (Yugoslavia) and voluntary (New York City) approaches to epidemic diseases like smallpox show that police-state tactics confer no advantage and probably exacerbate the problem. Finally, the U.S. Constitution, including the oft-abused "commerce clause," confers no federal authority to seize "emergency health powers"; even Philadelphia's horrendous yellow fever epidemic of 1793, which claimed nearly 10 percent of the city's population, was not regarded by the Founders as an excuse for a national "state of emergency"—despite the fact that Philadelphia was the nation's capital at the time, and the political leadership, including George Washington and Thomas Jefferson, fled the city.

The ongoing danger of biowarfare, both from terrorists and from hostile regimes, should not be ignored or discounted. But the proper solution is to trust the local, voluntary response, and not to use the threat of bioterrorism as an excuse to further erode American civil liberties or to unconstitutionally empower the federal government at the expense of state and local authority.

Periodical Bibliography

The following articles have been selected to supplement the diverse views presented in this chapter.

Bruce Berkowitz	"Information Warfare: Time to Prepare," *World & I*, January 2002.
Shannon Brownlee	"Return of an Old Scourge? Smallpox May Be the Deadliest Weapon in the Biowarfare Arsenal," *Washington Post*, November 26–December 2, 2002.
Don Feder	"Symposium: Q: Should Policymakers See Islam as an Enemy of the West? Yes: Islam Opposed to Western Ideals Such as Tolerance, Democracy and Civil Liberties," *Insight on the News*, November 5, 2001.
Maureen Freely	"The Ignorance of the Islamophobes," *New Statesman*, December 17, 2001.
Jerome Groopman	"Defending Against Bioterror," *Wall Street Journal*, October 17, 2001.
Pervez Hoodbhoy	"Muslims and the West: After September 11," *Free Inquiry*, Spring 2002.
Jack Miles	"Theology and the Clash of Civilizations," *Cross Currents*, Winter 2002.
Henry I. Miller	"Counter the Threat of Biological Weapons," *San Diego Union-Tribune*, September 26, 2001.
New Internationalist	"Islam: The Basics," May 2002.
Rachel Nowak	"Interview with Ken Alibek: Prepare for the Worst," *New Scientist*, July 14, 2001.
Ralph Peters	"Rolling Back Radical Islam," *Parameters*, Autumn 2002.
Ibn al-Rawandi	"Islam and Armageddon," *Free Inquiry*, Spring 2002.
Edward W. Said	"We All Swim Together," *New Statesman*, October 15, 2001.

CHAPTER 2

How Can National Security Best Be Enhanced?

Chapter Preface

After the September 11, 2001, terrorist attacks on America, many people wondered why the nation's intelligence community had not uncovered the plot ahead of time and done something to stop it. Political science professor Jack Citrin explains, "People are asking, 'why didn't [U.S. intelligence agencies] prevent this from happening? Were they asleep at the wheel?" *Time* magazine writers Massimo Calabresi and Romesh Ratnesar claim that "the CIA and the nation's other intelligence bureaucracy were caught flat-footed by the September 11 attack." Other commentators argued that it was unfair to blame the intelligence community for the attacks. Thomas Houlahan, director of the Military Assessment Program of the William R. Nelson Institute at James Madison University, asserts that "the CIA had been looking in the wrong direction in terms of threat assessment," a direction dictated by the administrations of Bill Clinton and George W. Bush. According to Houlahan, Clinton and Bush instructed the CIA to focus its attention on China, which they considered the most serious threat to national security. Despite conflicting theories of who was to blame for the September 11 attacks, most analysts agreed on two points: More needed to be done to enhance national security and a critical part of that effort must focus on the U.S. intelligence community. Reforms now being implemented at the CIA and FBI are both human and technological.

As Thomas Houlahan hinted, CIA intelligence gathering has continued to be mired in Cold War strategies that focus on nation-states such as Russia and China. However, many analysts believe that today the most serious threat to the nation's security is terrorism, not communism. The CIA has a host of agents who speak fluent Russian, but such agents are useless for infiltrating terrorist cells in the Middle East, where the dominant language is Arabic. Moreover, agents accustomed to conducting intelligence activities in large Russian cities have proven reluctant to live in the remote rural places where terrorists tend to establish their headquarters. This lack of covert human intelligence—which the intelligence community calls HUMINT—is now the focus of many of the reforms currently being implemented. In particular, the CIA is attempting to recruit individuals who speak Arabic.

Cold War methods have also resulted in a scarcity of signals intelligence—or, SIGINT. For example, the CIA is still relying on sophisticated technologies such as wiretaps, which proved effective during the Cold War but are largely inadequate in gaining intelligence from terrorist groups. After all, a conference room in the Kremlin can be wiretapped, but a cave in Afghanistan cannot. The CIA is now focusing its efforts on intercepting e-mails and other electronic communications, which the terrorists depend upon for planning attacks. Domestically, incompatible information technology systems have impeded communications between the agencies charged with national security: the State Department, the Immigration and Naturalization Service, and the FBI. If each agency could communicate readily with the others, critical pieces of information about certain individuals and their activities, which in discrete form might not appear worrisome, could, in aggregate, alert authorities to possible terrorist plots.

Focusing on HUMINT and SIGINT, the U.S. intelligence community is working on reforms in the hopes of preventing another September 11. In the following chapter, authors discuss other ways that national security can be enhanced. As is clear from examining the efforts of America's intelligence agencies, the solutions are likely to focus on both human and technological capabilities.

"We must spend what is necessary to protect our freedom, our security and prosperity."

Defense Spending Must Be Increased

Paul Wolfowitz

The September 11, 2001, terrorist attacks on America led to a reevaluation of the nation's defense capabilities and calls for increased military spending. Deputy Secretary of Defense Paul Wolfowitz contends in the following viewpoint, originally given as testimony before the Senate Appropriations Committee on February 27, 2002, that the United States must increase defense spending in order to protect Americans from new threats to national security. Arguing in support of President George W. Bush's proposed 2003 defense budget, which significantly increased defense spending, Wolfowitz claims that increased military funding is necessary to fight the war on terrorism, transform the military, and defend Americans from future threats. He maintains that defense budget cuts after the Cold War left the United States ill prepared for the dangers it now faces. Bush's defense budget was approved.

As you read, consider the following questions:

1. What five key areas will the increased defense budget address, as argued by Wolfowitz?
2. According to the author, what six key transformational goals define the military's highest priorities for investment in the years ahead?
3. How does the B-1 bomber illustrate the military's efforts to generate savings and efficiency, in the author's opinion?

Paul Wolfowitz, testimony before the Senate Appropriations Committee, Subcommittee on Defense in Washington, D.C., February 27, 2002.

O ne of the greatest and gravest changes was brought by [the September 11, 2001, terrorist attacks]—a day that changed our nation forever. September 11th has taught us once again that when it comes to America's defense, we must spend what is necessary to protect our freedom, our security and prosperity—not just for this generation, but to preserve peace and security for our children and our grandchildren.

Today, we are engaged in the enormous task of fighting a global war on terrorism. As difficult as it is to think about other challenges in the middle of waging this war, it is essential that we think beyond our current effort if we are to face the security challenges and conflicts that are certain to arise throughout this century.

Five Key Areas

The 2003 Defense Budget request is designed to address the President's goals in five key areas:
1. fighting and winning the war on terror;
2. defending the American people from a range of potential threats, from securing the homeland to defending against ballistic and cruise missiles;
3. restoring morale and readiness of the Armed Forces;
4. transforming the force and
5. managing the Defense Department in a more business-like manner.

Many elements of the budget address more than one of these goals. However, my remarks will focus largely on what we are doing to transform the force, a critical area in which we need Congress's help.

The Draw Down Went Too Far

When the Cold War ended, the United States began a very substantial draw down of our defense forces and our budgets. We cashed a large "peace dividend," lowering the level of our defense burden by half from the Cold War peak. Much of that was an appropriate adjustment to the great improvement in our security that resulted from the end of the Cold War. The draw down, however, ultimately went too far.

While our commitments around the world stayed the same and even grew in some cases, our country spent much of the 1990s living off investments made during the Cold War, instead of making new investments to address the threats of this new century. As I discussed with this committee [in 2001], even before September 11th, we faced the urgent need to replenish critical accounts. After September 11th, we find ourselves facing the additional challenges of accomplishing three significant missions at the same time. First, to win the global war on terrorism; second, to restore capabilities by making investments in procurement, people and modernization and third, to prepare for the future by accelerating the transformation for the 21st century.

It will be difficult and demanding to tackle all three of these missions at once, but we must do it—and without delay. Even as we fight the war on terror, potential adversaries study our methods and capabilities, and they plan for how they can take advantage of what they perceive to be our weaknesses and vulnerabilities. Now is precisely the moment we must begin to build forces that can frustrate those plans and provide us with the capabilities we need to win the wars of the coming decades.

We can only accomplish the Defense Department's three missions—fighting the war on terrorism, supporting our people and selectively modernizing the forces we have now, and transforming our Armed Forces for the wars of the future—with proper investments over a sustained period. And we must accomplish these missions in an environment of rising costs, particularly for that most critical element of the force—our people. Comparisons have been drawn between this budget request and those of the Cold War—but, it is important to consider that we simply could not buy the quality of people that comprise today's force, nor could we equip and train them properly at Cold War prices.

The 2003 budget addresses "must pay" bills such as retiree health care and pay raises ($14.1 billion)—if we don't pay our people properly, we risk losing this critical element of the force; and there are other bills such as realistic costing ($7.4 billion), inflation ($6.7 billion) and the war on terrorism ($19.4 billion). Added together, these bills come to $47.6 billion. That is why President Bush sent to Congress a 2003 defense budget request of $379 billion—a $48 billion increase from the 2002 budget, and the largest increase since the early 1980s.

New Defense Strategy

The 2003 budget request was guided by the results of [2001's] strategy review and the Quadrennial Defense Review (QDR), both of which involved an unprecedented degree of debate and discussion among the department's most senior leaders. Out of this intense debate, we reached agreement on the urgent need for real changes in our defense strategy.

I might add that our conclusions have not gone unnoticed. One foreign observer reports that the QDR contains "the most profound implications" of the four major defense reviews conducted since the end of the Cold War. What is most compelling about this analysis is that it appears in a Chinese journal. That Chinese observer thinks the QDR's conclusions are important as a blueprint for where we go from here—and we think so, too.

My statement addresses how the President's budget intends to meet this blueprint, shaped by the needs of the environment we face today and the environment we could face in the decades to come.

Among the new directions set in the QDR, the following are among the most important. First, we decided to move away from the two Major Theater War (MTW) force sizing construct, which called for maintaining forces capable of marching on and occupying the capitals of two adversaries and changing their regimes—at the same time. The new approach instead places greater emphasis on deterrence in four critical theaters, backed by the ability to swiftly defeat two aggressors at the same time, while preserving the option for one major offensive to occupy an aggressor's capital and replace the regime. By removing the requirement to maintain a second occupation force, we can free up resources for various lesser contingencies that might face us and also be able to invest for the future.

Second, to confront a world marked by surprise and substantial uncertainty, we agreed that we needed to shift our planning from the "threat-based" model that has guided our thinking in the past to a "capabilities-based" model for the future. We don't know who may threaten us or when or where. But, we do have some sense of what they may threaten us with and how. And we also have a sense of what capabilities can provide us important new advantages.

Third, this capabilities-based approach places great emphasis on defining where we want to go with the transformation of our forces. Transformation, as Secretary [of Defense Donald] Rumsfeld has said, "is about an awful lot more than bombs and bullets and dollars and cents; it's about new approaches, it's about culture, it's about mindset and ways of thinking of things."

Transformation Is Under Way

Even in just the few months of the current campaign, we have seen a great deal of that kind of change under way. To mention just one example, not long ago, an Air Force F-15 pilot had to be persuaded to forego a rated pilot's job to fly, instead, an unmanned Predator aircraft from a location far from the field of battle. For a pilot destined for the cockpit, it was a difficult choice for her—especially given concerns among some pilots that such an assignment could stymie their careers. But there is no question that unmanned vehicles have made a significant impact in the current campaign [against the ruling Taliban in Afghanistan] and promise even greater operational impacts in the future—which is why the Air Force leadership is working hard to encourage other such trailblazers to become Predator pilots and help define a new concept of operations. So, at this moment, what it means to be a fighter pilot in the U.S. Air Force is undergoing a transformation.

It is also important to note that transformation cannot mean transforming the entire force overnight. It begins with leveraging the systems we have with new technology and new thinking. As we begin by changing only a small percentage of the force we can, in fact, change the capability of the entire force.

That is our aim. And by giving some definition to what transformation is and putting money behind these ideas, we can energize the defense team in dramatic ways, and energize a transformation that will be ongoing and exponential.

Six Key Transformational Goals

We identified six key transformational goals that define our highest priorities for investments in the 2003–2007 Future Years Defense Program (FYDP).

First, to protect the U.S. homeland and forces overseas. Second, to project and sustain power in distant theaters. Third, to deny enemies sanctuary or places where they can hide and function. Fourth, to protect information networks from attack. Fifth, to use information technology to link up U.S. forces so they can fight jointly. And sixth, to maintain unhindered access to space—and protect U.S. space capabilities from enemy attack.

The U.S. Military Does Fantastically Well

Ever since the Berlin Wall fell, editorialists, politicians, and policy analysts have been pronouncing the United States military bloated, overpriced, mired in antiquated cold war assumptions, and unready for a "small wars" world. . . . Commentators across the spectrum agree that the military must abandon its fixation with heavy armor, big tactical aircraft, and other cold war relics in an effort to get lighter, faster, smaller, and more flexible. . . . By the time [President] George W. Bush took office, support for a capital-letters "Revolution in Military Affairs" (RMA) was so widespread—with Defense Secretary Donald Rumsfeld an especially strong advocate— that it looked like a military "transformation" might actually happen.

Thank goodness it didn't. Because a funny thing has happened since [the September 11, 2001, terrorist attacks]: The bloated, top-heavy, overpriced, cold war military has done fantastically well in [America's fight against terrorism].

Gregg Easterbrook, *New Republic*, December 17, 2001.

We reached these conclusions before September 11th, but our experiences since then have validated many of those conclusions, and reinforced the importance of continuing to move forward in these new directions. The 2003 budget request advances each of the six transformational goals by accelerating funding for the development of the transformational programs and by funding modernization programs that support transformation goals. . . .

Cost Savings

We have taken a realistic approach in looking at a number of programs and have found areas where we can save some money. We have proposed terminating a number of programs over the next five years that were not in line with the new defense strategy or were having program difficulties. These include the DD-21, Navy Area Missile Defense, 18 Army Legacy programs and the Peacekeeper Missile. We also accelerated retirement of a number of aging and expensive-to-maintain capabilities, such as the F-14, DD-963 destroyers and 1000 Vietnam-era helicopters.

We have focused modernization efforts on programs that support transformation. We restructured certain programs that were not meeting hurdles, such as the V-22 Osprey, Comanche and SBIRS programs. Regarding the V-22, the production rate has been slowed while attention is focused on correcting the serious technical problems identified by the blue ribbon panel and a rigorous flight test program is to be conducted to determine whether it is safe and reliable. The restructured programs reflect cost estimates and delivery dates that should be more realistic.

We are working to generate savings and efficiency in other programs as well. For example, the B-1 bomber cannot operate effectively in combat environment where there is a serious anti-aircraft threat. So the Air Force is reducing the B-1 bomber fleet by about one-third and using the savings to modernize the remaining aircraft with new precision weapons, self-protection systems and reliability upgrades that will make the B-1 suitable for future conflicts. This should add some $1.5 billion of advanced combat capability to today's aging B-1 fleet over the next five years—without requiring additional dollars from the taxpayers. These are the kinds of tradeoffs we are encouraging throughout the department. . . .

Ensuring Peace and Security

A budget of $379 billion represents a great deal of money. But, it is misleading to compare this budget to budgets of the Cold War or to the defense budgets of other countries. We do not face other countries' budgets on the battlefield; we fight their forces. The budget of the Taliban would have been a small fraction of that of the United States. Yet, it has been unquestionably important that we have had the capability to deploy forces rapidly and effectively to an unexpected theater of operations. Our success thus far in meeting this challenge only confirms that ours is the world's best military force. We need the world's best military force. We can't afford to have less than that.

The New York City comptroller's office estimated the local economic cost of the September 11th attacks on New York City alone will add up to about $100 billion over the next three years. The cost in human lives, and the pain and suffering of so many thousands of Americans who lost loved ones that day is incalculable.

The President's budget addresses our country's need to fight the war on terror, to support our men and women in uniform and modernize the forces we have and to prepare for the challenges of the 21st century. This committee is an important safeguard of the long-term interests of our great nation. We look forward to working with this committee to ensure that peace and security is what we can leave to generations to come.

> "It is best . . . to think of the Pentagon as a dangerously obese man. He should not be allowed to gorge further."

Defense Spending Is Too High

Paul Isaacs

In the aftermath of the September 11, 2001, terrorist attacks, many defense experts called for an increase in defense spending in order to prevent future attacks. Paul Isaacs argues in the following viewpoint that the United States already spends too much money on military weaponry. Arguing in opposition to President George W. Bush's 2003 defense budget, which significantly increased military spending, Isaacs claims that much of the money will be spent on obsolete weapons such as the Crusader, a howitzer that may have been useful during the Cold War but is far too ponderous for use in contemporary warfare. Isaacs contends that overblown budgets continue to be approved by legislators because representatives act in the interests of defense contractors, who donate liberally to congressional campaigns. Bush's defense budget was approved. Paul Isaacs writes for the *New Statesman*.

As you read, consider the following questions:
1. The U.S. defense budget is six times larger than what countries put together, as reported by Isaacs?
2. In the author's opinion, what is notable about the Fort Hood army base in Texas?
3. How much money did United Defense donate to Congress in 2001?

It is best, some people would suggest, to think of the Pentagon as a dangerously obese man. He should not be allowed to gorge further; he should be taken away from the table. As for President George W. Bush's five-year, $2.1 trillion (trn) defence spending deal, it may only forcefeed the patient until he explodes.

"Too much money has enabled the Pentagon to avoid reform and transformation," says John Isaacs, defence analyst for the Washington think-tank Council for a Livable World. "What it really needs is a ten-year diet."

The standard objection on the European left to Bush's bonanza budget can be summarised thus: money for development = good; $48 billion (bn) increase in defence spending = bad, very bad. Although many liberal critics in America think the same, some have a further complaint: namely, that the new budget is not just throwing a huge amount of money away on weaponry, but is throwing a huge amount away on the wrong kind of weaponry.

Obsolete Technology

So how exactly does the world's only remaining superpower use $2.1 trn in defence expenditure? What next for a country whose military budget was already six times larger than those of all the "axis of evil" countries combined [Iraq, Iran, and North Korea]—plus Cuba, Sudan and Syria thrown in for good measure? A weather machine?

What most critics agree on is the preponderance of heavy cold-war weaponry on the bill, at the expense of the Pentagon's proposed "transformation"—a strategy to reshape the army as a lighter, more deployable force.

The lion's share of [2003's] proposed $396.1bn defence budget will pay for controversial cold-war white elephants such as United Defense's Crusader howitzer, a tank-like vehicle designed to repel a Soviet invasion of Europe.

"The recent military build-up seems to have little to do with the actual threat," wrote the economist Paul Krugman in the *New York Times*, "unless you think [the terrorist group] al-Qaeda's next move will be a frontal assault by several heavily armoured vehicles."

Leaving obese men to one side, there is no better real-life

metaphor for military waste than the Fort Hood army base in central Texas. "It's the Grand Canyon of armour power," wrote the journalist William Greider in his 1998 investigation of military economics, *Fortress America: The American Military and the Consequences of Peace.*

Tucked in among Fort Hood's gentle prairie creeks and hills is one of the largest, deadliest and costliest displays of firepower on earth. Row upon row of tanks, trucks, missiles, helicopters and howitzers stretch in their hundreds, thousands, then tens of thousands, each pointing their way westwards into New Mexico, then infinity. "It's exhausting to behold," noted Greider, "but there's nothing else like it in the world."

Greider, a celebrated muckraker who has worked at *Rolling Stone* and the *Nation*, wasn't just writing copy for the US army, package holiday division. His interest in Fort Hood was not in the capability that rests there—more than 40 per cent of US army forces—but in how, for most of the time, and at a cost of millions, that was all it was doing: resting. In effect, Fort Hood's magnificent vistas represent nothing more than a dumping ground for the world's most advanced fighting technology. And if critics are correct about the waste in Bush's budget, those vistas will be getting wider and more magnificent as the years go on.

The base's thousands of M-1 Abrams tanks, for example— "Cadillacs with guns", the soldiers call them—were used to devastating effect during the Gulf war against [Iraqi leader] Saddam Hussein's much inferior forces, but there is little place for them in this era of Afghanistan-style in-and-out bombings.

In fact, so devastating is this newer form of air warfare that it is little wonder the Bush administration is feeling so cocky about downing [Hussein's] regime right now. Following the Soviet crash in 1991, no state in the world has the same capacity for military research and design as the United States.

Better Safe than Sorry

Since the cold war, Pentagon spending has always been based on the premise that it is better to be safe than sorry. Why build 1,000 nuclear warheads—enough to bring about a nuclear winter—when you can build 6,000? The city of Los Angeles may have 1.4 million "food-insecure" (Californian for "hungry") people in 2002, but the army still gets to spend $48bn this year on the Commanche, a modernised version of a helicopter that hasn't been useful since the Korean war.

2003 Spending on Military Boondoggles

- V-22 Osprey ($26 billion): This vertical take-off aircraft has killed 30 soldiers just in the testing phase.
- DDG-51 Destroyer ($2.7 billion): Designed during the cold war to fight the Soviet navy. Where are they now?
- B-61 "Bunker Busting" Nuclear Bomb (undisclosed sum): Because what the world really needs now is a new nuclear weapon.
- Anti-Ballistic Missile Defence ($11 billion): More than 20 years in the making and it still won't work.
- F-22 Raptor ($5.2 billion): Little improvement on the F-16 —which has no peer in the world—and said to be less effective than the in-production F-18.

Paul Isaacs, *New Statesman*, March 25, 2002.

In the air, the only way the US could come up against an enemy with a plane as powerful as the F-16 would be by selling it to them. But this hasn't stopped Bush approving $12bn for three further jets—the Joint Strike Fighter, the F-18 Super Hornet and the F-22 Raptor—and for a redesign of the F-16. And that's only this year's costs; in the next half-decade, spending on the four fighters will increase to hundreds of billions.

The Crusader White Elephant

The Crusader howitzer, which got a $475.2 million (m) payout this year, is one of the most contentious weapons in the budget, and a good example of what's wrong with it. The system consists of two parts: the howitzer weapon itself, a cannon-like barrel that fires between ten and 12 rounds a minute over a distance of 40km; and the resupply vehicle, which carries it across the battlefield. Both weigh a svelte 40 tons, making Crusader one of the deadliest—but also heaviest and slowest—mobile artillery weapons in existence.

But does anyone need it? On current evidence, future conflicts will provide scant openings for a slowcoach like Crusader. The Pentagon says battles are more likely to be dispersed over a large area, using unmanned vehicles and swift bombing raids (or "drive-by shootings", as the army calls them). Speed is all nowadays: just imagine how long it would take Crusader to get to Baghdad—more than 7,000 miles from the US—and that depends on finding a plane big enough to carry it. At the moment, the only jets capable of doing the job are the C-5 and the mammoth C-15 (aka "the flying truck"), and neither is in plentiful supply.

"To call Crusader a white elephant is an insult to white elephants," says Conn Hallinan, a columnist on military affairs for the *San Francisco Examiner*. "You can't fit it in a plane, it breaks any bridge it crosses, and you couldn't get it to Afghanistan on a dare."

A Boon to Defense Companies and Congressmen

So how does an obsolete weapon like Crusader get approved, let alone built and deployed? Because it creates jobs and security for thousands of people—not least defence companies and congressmen. When Oklahoma Representative J.C. Watts said he was "obviously sold" on Crusader last year, it wasn't just because he felt the howitzer was a really decent idea. A factory in Elgin, in Watts's district, will build parts for Crusader, ensuring his constituents hundreds of jobs—and his campaign thousands of votes. And in 2000, Watts was given $6,250 in contributions by United Defense's parent company, the Carlyle Group.

In [2001] alone, United Defense has donated $62,750 to Congress. That might be small beer compared to Lockheed Martin ($900,000) or Philip Morris ($1m), but as far as political bribes go, it's enough to get things moving. Scratch wherever there's a factory making Crusader parts, and you'll almost certainly find a donation to the local congressperson from either Carlyle or United Defense, even if it's a measly thousand bucks.

The trick is to spread weapons sub-contractors out into as many congressional districts across the US as possible; that way, if the contract for a weapon of ambiguous use is questioned in Congress, it helps no end if thousands of congressmen's constituents are building different parts of it.

No defence company will willingly cancel its own contract. So the decision as to whether a weapon should be kept rests with the Pentagon accounting offices. For a bureau that regularly "misplaces" hundreds of billions of dollars, this is rarely helpful.

A study of the Crusader is instructive. Two years ago, George W. Bush claimed Crusader was "too heavy" and "not lethal enough", in effect rejecting the programme in favour of the transformation. In April 2001, an advisory panel appointed by the secretary of defence, Donald Rumsfeld, actually recommended that Congress cancel Crusader and a host of others like it. At that point, it appeared, nothing would save the system, not even the presence in the Carlyle Group of George Bush Sr.

All that changed after [the September 11, 2001, terrorist attacks]. No one wanted to be seen as anything so wimpish as a dove anymore, so the Pentagon dutifully renewed almost all of its weapons contracts, including Crusader. With the new funding taken into account, government spending on the howitzer amounts to $1.8bn since 1994. That's a phenomenal price for a weapon that even the president doesn't want. Unfortunately, it's not the only one.

"The aftermath of the 11th has compounded all the problems in military spending," Greider [said]. "The Bush team decided the window provided by a 'wartime presidency' was too good to pass up. By creating a high state of national alarm over an openended threat, it justifies not only endless armaments, but also a newly empowered national-security state." That isn't just fighting terrorism, Greider speculates—"It's empire building." [*Editor's note:* George W. Bush's 2003 defense budget was approved.]

"The threat posed by ballistic missiles armed with weapons of mass destruction exists and promises to intensify."

America Needs a Missile Defense System

Jim Garamone

In the following viewpoint Jim Garamone contends that America needs a ballistic missile defense system to protect itself from hostile enemies. According to Garamone, several nations have developed or are developing ballistic missiles armed with weapons of mass destruction that could be used to harm the United States. He claims that a missile defense system would protect the nation from these and as-yet unknown threats to national security. Jim Garamone writes for the American Forces Press Service, an information source for the U.S. military.

As you read, consider the following questions:
1. What attack was the first use of ballistic missiles against the United States, as reported by Garamone?
2. In CIA director George Tenet's opinion, what nations pose a growing missile threat to the United States?
3. From what country does Iran get much of its missile technology, according to the author?

Jim Garamone, "Why America Needs Missile Defense," American Forces Press Service, August 17, 2001.

The United States is ready to spend billions on ballistic missile defense. The question many critics have is whether the threat warrants the investment.

"Right now some 28 countries have ballistic missiles, they are of different ranges, they have various warheads, they have various ways to launch them," Defense Secretary Donald H. Rumsfeld said recently. That number will only go up.

Ballistic Missiles: Then and Now

The threat exists, and Americans have been on the receiving end for almost 60 years. It started when the Nazis launched hundreds of V-2 rockets against Britain and Allied forces in Europe during the closing months of World War II. More recently, 28 Americans died and 98 others were wounded when an Iraqi Scud missile struck a barracks in Dhahran, Saudi Arabia, during the 1991 Persian Gulf War.

Those weapons used conventional warheads, but future missiles could be tipped with weapons of mass destruction. Iraq had adapted some of its Scuds to carry chemical weapons and had started a nuclear weapons program before the Gulf War.

The idea of a country like Iraq with nuclear bombs shouldn't be startling. The technology and know-how behind the World War II atom bombs are 60 years old, so all any nation or party needs for a nuclear weapons program today are resources and the inclination. The image of a nuclear missile strike against the United States or U.S. forces, even with a primitive Hiroshima-type bomb, is as terrifying now as it was in 1945.

There are threats today that we know of. The point of missile defense is, we can't say with any certainty where the threats of the future will come from. A variety of states and groups continue to seek to acquire weapons of mass destruction and the means to deliver them.

The Known Threats

CIA Director George Tenet testified before Congress in February [2001] about the growing missile threat. "We continue to face ballistic missile threats from a variety of actors beyond Russia and China—specifically, North Korea, probably Iran, and possibly Iraq," he said.

"In some cases, their programs are the result of indigenous technological development, and in other cases, they are the beneficiaries of direct foreign assistance," he continued. "While these emerging programs involve far fewer missiles with less accuracy, yield, survivability and reliability than those we faced during the Cold War, they still pose a threat to U.S. interests."

[In 1998], North Korea tested its Taepo Dong-1 rocket, which could be converted into an intercontinental ballistic missile (ICBM). The missile would be capable of delivering a small biological or chemical weapon to the U.S. mainland. The follow-on Taepo Dong-2 could deliver a nuclear payload to the United States.

Defenseless Against Mortal Danger

On September 11, 2001, our nation's enemies attacked us using hijacked airliners. Next time, the vehicles of death and destruction might well be ballistic missiles armed with nuclear, chemical, or biological warheads. And let us be clear: The United States is defenseless against this mortal danger. We would today have to suffer helplessly a ballistic missile attack, just as we suffered helplessly on September 11. But the dead would number in the millions and a constitutional crisis would likely ensue, because the survivors would wonder—with good reason—if their government were capable of carrying out its primary constitutional duty: to "provide for the common defense."

Brian T. Kennedy, *Vital Speeches*, January 1, 2002.

Tenet said Iran has one of the largest and most capable ballistic missile programs in the Middle East. "(Iran's) public statements suggest that it plans to develop longer-range rockets for use in a space-launch program, but Tehran could follow the North Korean pattern and test an ICBM capable of delivering a light payload to the United States in the next few years," he said.

"And given the likelihood that Iraq continues its missile development work, we think that it, too, could develop an ICBM capability sometime in the next decade, assuming it received foreign assistance."

The ICBM threat is in the future. The threat from short-range and medium-range ballistic missiles is here now. Deployed U.S. forces must be able to defend against this threat. Iraq's Scud, North Korea's No-Dong missile, Iran's Shahab-3, Pakistan's Ghauri and the Indian Agni II could pose significant threats.

The countries themselves might not launch the missiles. Their sales of these technologies to others could pose risks in the future. "Russian entities [in 2001] continued to supply a variety of ballistic missile-related goods and technical know-how to countries such as Iran, India, China and Libya," Tenet said. "Indeed, the transfer of ballistic missile technology from Russia to Iran was substantial . . . and in our judgment will continue to accelerate Iranian efforts to develop new missiles and to become self-sufficient in production."

In turn, Iran may sell its newfound expertise to a third party. "Chinese missile-related technical assistance to foreign countries also has been significant over the years. Chinese help has enabled Pakistan to move rapidly toward serial production of solid-propellant missiles," Tenet said. "In addition to Pakistan, firms in China provided missile-related items, raw materials or other help to several countries of proliferation concern, including Iran, North Korea and Libya."

China has reiterated its commitment to curb sales of missile technology. "Based on what we know about China's past proliferation behavior, . . . we are watching and analyzing carefully for any sign that Chinese entities may be acting against that commitment," Tenet said.

These countries are some of the known threats today. Where will the threat come from tomorrow? Rumsfeld has said U.S. strategy should be "capability-based" in the future. This means the United States should have the means to combat any threat, no matter what it is or where it originates. Further, U.S. research, development and testing should expand to include defenses against cruise missiles.

The threat posed by ballistic missiles armed with weapons of mass destruction exists and promises to intensify. Rumsfeld's repeated position is that the United States doing nothing to protect its population from such a threat could be tragically wrong.

> *"Any country that is capable of building a long-range missile . . . would also have the capability and motivation to build effective countermeasures to the planned defense."*

A Missile Defense System Would Not Protect America

David Wright and Theodore Postol

According to David Wright and Theodore Postol in the following viewpoint, an effective ballistic missile defense system is technologically infeasible. They claim that the defense system currently being developed by the U.S. military can be easily foiled using such countermeasures as disguising a warhead in an aluminum-coated Mylar balloon. In Wright's and Postol's opinion, the U.S. government is wasting money on a national defense system that may actually make America less safe. Wright is a physicist and Postol is a professor of science, technology, and national security policy at the Massachusetts Institute of Technology.

As you read, consider the following questions:
1. How do the authors define "inherent asymmetry" in regards to missile defense?
2. As defined by Wright and Postol, what are "bomblets"?
3. What are the two parts of the missile defense problem, according to the authors?

David Wright and Theodore Postol, "Missile Defense Won't Work," *Boston Globe*, May 11, 2000. Copyright © 2000 by *Boston Globe*. Reproduced by permission of Copyright Clearance Center, Inc.

The United States is on the verge of deploying a national missile defense system intended to shoot down long-range missiles. The Clinton administration is scheduled to decide this fall [2000] whether to give the green light to a system that is expected to cost more than $60 billion, sour relations with Russia and China, and block deep cuts in nuclear arsenals.[1]

But the real scandal is that the defense being developed won't work—and few in Washington seem to know or care.

An Easily Defeated System

The chief difficulty in trying to develop missile defenses is not getting vast systems of complex hardware to work as intended—although that is a daunting task. The key problem is that the defense has to work against an enemy who is trying to foil the system. What's worse, the attacker can do so with technology much simpler than the technology needed for the defense system. This inherent asymmetry means the attacker has the advantage despite the technological edge the United States has over a potential attacker such as North Korea.

We recently completed, along with nine other scientists, a yearlong study that examined in detail what countermeasures an emerging missile state could take to defeat the missile defense system the United States is planning. That study shows that effective countermeasures require technology much less sophisticated than is needed to build a long-range missile in the first place—technology that would be available to the potential attacker. This kind of analysis is possible since the United States has already selected the interceptor and sensor technologies its defense system would use. We assessed the full missile defense system the United States is planning—not just the first phase planned for 2005—and assumed only that it is constrained by the laws of physics.

We examined three countermeasures in detail, each of which would defeat the planned US defense.

A country that decided to deliver biological weapons by ballistic missile could divide the lethal agent into 100 or more

---

1. Bill Clinton elected to leave the issue for his successor, George W. Bush, to decide. Bush went ahead with the deployment.

small bombs, known as "bomblets," as a way of dispersing the agent over the target. This would also overwhelm the defense, which couldn't shoot at so many warheads.

The Rumsfeld panel, a high-level commission convened by Congress in 1998 to assess the ballistic missile threat to the United States [named after now–Secretary of Defense Donald Rumsfeld], noted that potential attackers could build such bomblets. We show this in detail.

Ballistic Missiles Are the Least Likely Vehicles

There are ways to hurt the US that do not involve the launch of intercontinental ballistic missiles. Even nuclear weapons could be delivered in many ways, for instance by using trucks or freighters or . . . ship-launched short-range missiles. But the intercontinental ballistic missile is not just one among the many vehicles that might be used by terrorists or a rogue state to attack us with nuclear weapons—*it is the least likely vehicle*. Though some terrorists are willing to commit suicide in their attacks, the heads of the nations that harbor them never have been. The leaders of the Taliban [Afghanistan's ruling regime in 2001] did not publicly acknowledge that the September 11 [2001, terrorist] attacks were organized in Afghanistan, and [Libyan leader Mohammar] Qaddafi has never admitted that the explosion of a Pan American airliner over Lockerbie was planned in Libya.

But unlike such terrorist attacks, an attack by intercontinental ballistic missiles carries an indelible return address. Every launch of such missiles is inevitably detected and its source identified by the fleet of American Defense Support Program satellites. Even granting that a state like North Korea or Iraq might eventually be able to deploy nuclear-armed intercontinental missiles, why would any head of government, however much he may hate us, attack us with intercontinental ballistic missiles, or allow terrorists on his soil to launch such an attack, when he and they could use many other means to deliver nuclear weapons anonymously?

Steven Weinberg, *New York Review*, February 14, 2002.

An attacker launching missiles with nuclear weapons would have other options. It could disguise the warhead by enclosing it in an aluminum-coated Mylar balloon and releasing it with a large number of empty balloons. None of the missile defense sensors could tell which balloon held the warhead, and again the defense could not shoot at all of them.

Alternately, we showed that the warhead could be enclosed in a thin shroud cooled with liquid nitrogen—a common laboratory material—so it would be invisible to the heat-seeking interceptors the defense will use.

These are only three of many possible countermeasures. And none of these ideas is new; most are as old as ballistic missiles themselves.

Ignoring the Problem

How is it possible that this problem is being ignored? The Pentagon, saying it must walk before it can run, has divided the missile defense problem into two parts: getting the system to work against missiles without realistic countermeasures and then hoping to get it to work against missiles with countermeasures. Few doubt the first step could eventually be done, but such "walking" would be useless against an actual attack by North Korea or any other country.

The second step—getting the defense to work against countermeasures—is the one that matters. And our study showed in detail that the planned defense won't be able to do this.

Unfortunately, the debate in Washington revolves around only the first step. The Pentagon plans to determine the "technological readiness" of the system [during the summer of 2000] after three tests that lack realistic countermeasures. And President [Bill] Clinton's decision whether to deploy will be based on that assessment. The deployment decision is simply being made on the wrong criteria.

This situation is similar to a group of people deciding to build a bridge to the moon. Instead of assessing the feasibility of the full project before moving forward, they decide to start building the onramps, since that's the part they know how to do.

The reality is that any country that is capable of building a long-range missile and has the motivation to launch it against the United States would also have the capability and motivation to build effective countermeasures to the planned defense. To assume otherwise is to base defense planning on wishful thinking.

> *"[Iran, Iraq, and North Korea] constitute an axis of evil, arming to threaten the peace of the world."*

America Must Confront the Threat Posed by Iran, Iraq, and North Korea

George W. Bush

In the following viewpoint, originally given as a State of the Union Address in 2002, just four months after the September 11, 2001, terrorist attacks on America, President George W. Bush argues that Iran, Iraq, and North Korea pose a serious threat to the nation's security. According to Bush, these nations have been developing weapons of mass destruction, which they could eventually provide to terrorists for use against the United States. In light of these facts, he maintains, America must not wait for these dangerous regimes to amass more weapons but must actively stop the proliferation. In the spring of 2003, the United States went to war with Iraq and successfully deposed the regime.

As you read, consider the following questions:

1. According to Bush, what did the United States find in Afghanistan that confirmed America's worst fears?
2. What groups are part of a terrorist underworld, as cited by Bush?
3. What specific actions on the part of Iran, Iraq, and North Korea lead the president to think these nations pose a serious threat?

George W. Bush, State of the Union Address, January 29, 2002.

A s we gather tonight, our nation is at war [with Afghani-stan to fight terrorism], our economy is in recession, and the civilized world faces unprecedented dangers. Yet the state of our Union has never been stronger.

September 11 and the War Against Terrorism

We last met in an hour of shock and suffering. In four short months, our nation has comforted the victims [of the September 11, 2001, terrorist attacks on America], begun to rebuild New York and the Pentagon, rallied a great coalition, captured, arrested, and rid the world of thousands of terrorists, destroyed Afghanistan's terrorist training camps, saved a people from starvation, and freed a country from brutal oppression.

The American flag flies again over our embassy in Kabul [Afghanistan]. Terrorists who once occupied Afghanistan now occupy cells at Guantanamo Bay [Cuba]. And terrorist leaders who urged followers to sacrifice their lives are running for their own.

America and Afghanistan are now allies against terror. We'll be partners in rebuilding that country. . . .

The last time we met in this chamber, the mothers and daughters of Afghanistan were captives in their own homes, forbidden from working or going to school. Today women are free, and are part of Afghanistan's new government. . . .

Our progress is a tribute to the spirit of the Afghan people, to the resolve of our coalition, and to the might of the United States military. When I called our troops into action, I did so with complete confidence in their courage and skill. And tonight, thanks to them, we are winning the war on terror. The men and women of our Armed Forces have delivered a message now clear to every enemy of the United States: Even 7,000 miles away, across oceans and continents, on mountaintops and in caves—you will not escape the justice of this nation.

For many Americans, these four months have brought sorrow, and pain that will never completely go away. Every day a retired firefighter returns to Ground Zero [where the World Trade Center towers collapsed on September 11], to feel closer to his two sons who died there. At a memorial in New York, a little boy left his football with a note for his lost father: Dear Daddy, please take this to heaven. I don't want to play football until I can play with you again some day.

[In December 2001], at the grave of her husband, Michael, a CIA officer and Marine who died in Mazur-e-Sharif, Shannon Spann said these words of farewell: "Semper Fi, my love.". . .

Our cause is just, and our country will never forget the debt we owe Michael and all who gave their lives for freedom.

Confirming Dire Fears

Our cause is just, and it continues. Our discoveries in Afghanistan confirmed our worst fears, and showed us the true scope of the task ahead. We have seen the depth of our enemies' hatred in videos, where they laugh about the loss of innocent life. And the depth of their hatred is equaled by the madness of the destruction they design. We have found diagrams of American nuclear power plants and public water facilities, detailed instructions for making chemical weapons, surveillance maps of American cities, and thorough descriptions of landmarks in America and throughout the world.

What we have found in Afghanistan confirms that, far from ending there, our war against terror is only beginning. Most of the 19 men who hijacked planes on September the 11th were trained in Afghanistan's camps, and so were tens of thousands of others. Thousands of dangerous killers, schooled in the methods of murder, often supported by outlaw regimes, are now spread throughout the world like ticking time bombs, set to go off without warning.

Thanks to the work of our law enforcement officials and coalition partners, hundreds of terrorists have been arrested. Yet, tens of thousands of trained terrorists are still at large. These enemies view the entire world as a battlefield, and we must pursue them wherever they are. So long as training camps operate, so long as nations harbor terrorists, freedom is at risk. And America and our allies must not, and will not, allow it.

Shutting Down Regimes That Support Terrorism

Our nation will continue to be steadfast and patient and persistent in the pursuit of two great objectives. First, we will shut down terrorist camps, disrupt terrorist plans, and bring terrorists to justice. And, second, we must prevent the terrorists and regimes who seek chemical, biological or nuclear weapons from threatening the United States and the world.

Our military has put the terror training camps of Afghanistan out of business, yet camps still exist in at least a dozen countries. A terrorist underworld—including groups like Hamas, Hezbollah, Islamic Jihad, Jaish-i-Mohammed—operates in remote jungles and deserts, and hides in the centers of large cities.

Earning the Description "Axis of Evil"

To listen to critics of Pres. [George W.] Bush's "Axis of Evil" speech, you would think he just picked three nations out of a hat. However, the three he named—Iraq, Iran, and North Korea—have earned the description. All boast dictatorial, terrorist regimes that are overtly hostile to U.S. interests. All squander critical national resources to develop weapons of mass destruction, with America as their most probable target. Moreover, although they don't represent an "axis" in the sense that Italy, Japan, and Germany did in World War II, they increasingly cooperate with each other to coordinate their opposition to the U.S. and its ideals of freedom and equality.

Jack Spencer, *USA Today Magazine*, May 2002.

While the most visible military action is in Afghanistan, America is acting elsewhere. We now have troops in the Philippines, helping to train that country's armed forces to go after terrorist cells that have executed an American, and still hold hostages. Our soldiers, working with the Bosnian government, seized terrorists who were plotting to bomb our embassy. Our Navy is patrolling the coast of Africa to block the shipment of weapons and the establishment of terrorist camps in Somalia.

My hope is that all nations will heed our call, and eliminate the terrorist parasites who threaten their countries and our own. Many nations are acting forcefully. Pakistan is now cracking down on terror, and I admire the strong leadership of President [Pervez] Musharraf.

But some governments will be timid in the face of terror. And make no mistake about it: If they do not act, America will.

The Axis of Evil

Our second goal is to prevent regimes that sponsor terror from threatening America or our friends and allies with weapons of mass destruction. Some of these regimes have been pretty quiet since September the 11th. But we know their true nature. North Korea is a regime arming with missiles and weapons of mass destruction, while starving its citizens.

Iran aggressively pursues these weapons and exports terror, while an unelected few repress the Iranian people's hope for freedom.

Iraq continues to flaunt its hostility toward America and to support terror. The Iraqi regime has plotted to develop anthrax, and nerve gas, and nuclear weapons for over a decade. This is a regime that has already used poison gas to murder thousands of its own citizens—leaving the bodies of mothers huddled over their dead children. This is a regime that agreed to international inspections—then kicked out the inspectors. This is a regime that has something to hide from the civilized world.

States like these, and their terrorist allies, constitute an axis of evil, arming to threaten the peace of the world. By seeking weapons of mass destruction, these regimes pose a grave and growing danger. They could provide these arms to terrorists, giving them the means to match their hatred. They could attack our allies or attempt to blackmail the United States. In any of these cases, the price of indifference would be catastrophic.

We will work closely with our coalition to deny terrorists and their state sponsors the materials, technology, and expertise to make and deliver weapons of mass destruction. We will develop and deploy effective missile defenses to protect America and our allies from sudden attack. And all nations should know: America will do what is necessary to ensure our nation's security.

We'll be deliberate, yet time is not on our side. I will not wait on events, while dangers gather. I will not stand by, as peril draws closer and closer. The United States of America will not permit the world's most dangerous regimes to threaten us with the world's most destructive weapons.

Our war on terror is well begun, but it is only begun. This campaign may not be finished on our watch—yet it must be and it will be waged on our watch.

We can't stop short. If we stop now—leaving terror camps intact and terror states unchecked—our sense of security would be false and temporary. History has called America and our allies to action, and it is both our responsibility and our privilege to fight freedom's fight.

"None of the 'axis' states [Iran, Iraq, and North Korea] is behind [the terrorist group] Al Qaeda. This is a new force in the world."

Focusing on Iran, Iraq, and North Korea Threatens National Security

Llewellyn D. Howell

Llewellyn D. Howell argues in the following viewpoint that contrary to President George W. Bush's claims, Iran, Iraq, and North Korea do not constitute an "axis of evil." Countering assertions Bush made in his 2002 State of the Union Address, delivered just four months after the September 11, 2001, terrorist attacks on America, Howell claims that these nations are not working together to provide terrorists with weapons of mass destruction that could be used against the United States. Indeed, Howell claims, to focus on these nations is to ignore the real threat to America's security: terrorist groups such as al-Qaeda, the group responsible for the September 11 attacks. Howell, International Affairs Editor of *USA Today*, is director of executive MBA programs, College of Business Administration, University of Hawaii, Manoa.

As you read, consider the following questions:
1. What effect has Bush's use of the term "evil" had on the battle against terrorism, in Howell's opinion?
2. According to the author, what is the only linear relationship between Iran, Iraq, and North Korea?

I s it enough that a silly phrase, an "Axis of Evil," has been beaten to death by adversaries and allies? Hardly. There can be no limit on what can be said about this inappropriate and misconceived characterization of what was intended to be the central foreign policy theme of the Bush Administration.[1]

The Problem with Evil

Both ends of the simplistic phrase deserve as much attention as we can give it. Let's start with the designation of "evil" for the three countries named—Iran, Iraq, and North Korea. Until [the September 11, 2001, terrorist attacks on America], evil was something you found in third-rate movies and in churches from the dark side of Christianity. Evil has to do with the devil, the supernatural, and divergent religious beliefs that underlie subcultures. Evil is propagated by the devil, that grotesque figure conjured up with ghosts and demons by true believers. It plays on the most primitive instincts of mankind in calling together those who fear the earthly manifestations of the spirits of Hades.

By branding the conflict one between good and evil, Bush has brought religion to the battle with terrorism. While arguing that the current conflict is one with a radical subgroup and not with Islam, the President, with his axis of evil analogy, nevertheless calls upon conservative Judeo-Christian sensitivities to rally the nation (and a few others) behind his cause. The inclusion of the concept of evil incorporates religion, underpinning the notion that this is a clash of cultures and that ultimately this is a war between civilizations— Judeo-Christianity vs. Islam.

The Administration's argument might be more plausible if the three named nations had something in common that could realistically be labeled evil, but they don't. Iran's positioning for the last 23 years has clearly been one of having an alternative religious foundation to that of the Judeo-Christian West. Being driven by powerful and recognized beliefs that are at variance with those of the West is not evil.

---

1. In President George W. Bush's 2002 State of the Union Address, he referred to Iran, Iraq, and North Korea as an "Axis of Evil" because they were purportedly amassing weapons of mass destruction that they could eventually provide to terrorists.

Saddam Hussein of Iraq, from a political science point of view, would better be identified as a criminal tribalist than as evil. North Korea's monarchic and dictatorial leader, Kim Jong-Il, is frequently portrayed as a psychologically unbalanced loner, out of touch with the reality of the modern world. If this is evil, we have thousands of institutions (and many more households) filled with evil people right here in America. Iran is a religious state built around the premises of Shi'a Islam. Iraq is a secular government, albeit Sunni Islam in most of its personnel. North Korea is an antireligious system with operations more akin to thuggery than to organized political opposition. What the three states have in common is a willingness to flout U.S. policy more than any strain of underlying evil.

Very Lame Geometry

The use of the term "axis" is a gimmick to bring the U.S. effort into comparison with the vastly different circumstances of World War II. There is more to having allies than just a common enemy. The World War II Axis involved several characteristics that set it off as a bloc. Germany, Italy, and Japan had common authoritarian political systems and similar centralized economic ones. They saw themselves as cooperating in a war effort against the Western Europeans and the U.S. German and Italian troops fought together, and German troops even fought on Italian soil. Iran, Iraq, and North Korea have no such trait or any willingness to work together. Equating the World War II Axis and the grouping of the two Middle East rivals and an Asian megalomaniac is like equating plywood and sawdust. One is missing its most important ingredient—glue.

There is no glue among the three rogue states. The only linear relationship the three have is their willingness to defy U.S. dictates and to seek every means to undermine American hegemony in the world order, including the use of weapons of mass destruction. If this is the source of linearity, there may well be other states—especially in the Islamic world—that are similarly inclined, but just don't have the physical capabilities yet. In addition to the evil three, Russia, China, Syria, and Libya have been named as potential targets of U.S. nuclear weapons—maybe even with preemptive strikes—if they become threats to American civilization in the way made imaginable by the World Trade Center and Pentagon attacks.

Fictitious Triumvirate

The blatant truth of the matter is that not one of those states [Iran, Iraq, and North Korea] had anything to do with the September 11 [2001, terrorist] attacks, let alone all three being part of some triumvirate Bush labels the "axis of evil." Iran hates Iraq and vice-versa. In fact, it's more likely that they'd be plotting the destruction of one another before they bothered with the U.S.—while North Korea has nothing much to do with any other country, let alone Iran and Iraq.

Carlos Kelly, Democraticunderground.com, February 1, 2002.

"Axis" in this circumstance looks like very lame geometry. If not simply disconnected and isolated dots in the galaxy of peoples and states that are challenging the U.S., the three could at best be described as a "V of potentially violent contrariness" in the international system—no axis and not evil.

Misplaced Focus

One of the most threatening consequences of the use of an axis of evil as an organizing concept is the fact that it focuses on nation-states as the object of foreign policy. If anything was learned from Sept. 11, it should be the fact that the old world of realist foreign policy is gone. While nation-states like North Korea still must be dealt with, it's clear that they can be dealt with. We can deter, defend against, and even defeat Iraq, Russia, or Syria.[2] Dealing with the subterranean and conspiratorial zealots of [the terrorist group] Al Qaeda is a horse of a different color, a different dimension than the World War II partners in global criminality. The axis of evil concept dismisses the thought of Al Qaeda as an independent movement, with roots far deeper than the political ideologies that have been witness to the wars of political worlds that came to represent the 20th century.

2. In 2003, the United States invaded Iraq, quickly toppling leader Saddam Hussein's regime.

None of the "axis" states is behind Al Qaeda. This is a new force in the world. Our usual weapons, offensive or defensive, cannot be applied. This is a force that cannot be threatened with death or destruction. The threat of death is meaningless to a suicide bomber or a suicide organization, so World War II concepts not only don't fit the need for strategy, they mislead. They provide a sense of complacency when none should exist. The war against Al Qaeda has to be one made infamous in the Vietnam War—that of "hearts and minds," not physical destruction. The weapons against this enemy have to be communication and socialization, not bunker bombs and antiballistic missiles.

Periodical Bibliography

The following articles have been selected to supplement the diverse views presented in this chapter.

Joseph Cirincione	"The Persistence of the Missile Defense Illusion," Carnegie Endowment for International Peace, July 2–4, 1998, www.ceip.org.
Gregg Easterbrook	"Force of Habit—In Defense of a Bloated Military," *New Republic*, December 17, 2001.
Michael Eisenstadt	"Curtains for the Ba'ath," *National Interest*, Winter 2001/2002.
Larry Everest	"Creating Pretexts: The Campaign Against Iraq," *Z Magazine*, April 2002.
Brian T. Kennedy	"Protecting Our Nation: The Urgent Need for Ballistic Missile Defense," *Vital Speeches*, January 1, 2002.
Robert J. Lieber	"Containment Has Run Its Course," *Los Angeles Times*, September 29, 2002.
Michael O'Hanlon	"Cruise Control: A Case for Missile Defense," *National Interest*, Spring 2002.
Theodore Postol	"Why Missile Defense Won't Work," *Technology Review*, April 2002.
Daniel Smith	"The Ballistic Missile Threat," Center for Defense Information, 2000, www.cdi.org.
John Spratt Jr. and Hugh Brady	"National Security vs. Social Security: Is the Defense Budget Sustainable?" *Brookings Review*, Summer 2002.
Pete Stark	"Opposing Military Force Against Iraq," *People's Weekly World*, October 19, 2002.
Mark Thompson	"The Lessons of Afghanistan," *Time*, February 18, 2002.
Wanderer	"War and Weakness," September 12, 2002.
Steven Weinberg	"Can Missile Defense Work?" *New York Review of Books*, February 14, 2002.

CHAPTER 3

How Should the United States Respond to Terrorism?

Chapter Preface

After the September 11, 2001, terrorist attacks, airplanes, once symbols of an affluent and mobile America, became associated in many people's minds with death and destruction. Indeed, news footage of two commercial airliners crashing into the World Trade Center became proof of the nation's vulnerability to terrorism. Unsurprisingly, the attacks prompted urgent calls to protect the nation from further terrorist acts, and the first item on most people's list was enhancing airport security. Responding to the challenge, in November 2001 President George W. Bush signed legislation creating the Transportation Security Administration (TSA), which makes the federal government responsible for security at the nation's airports.

Under the old system the airlines provided security. Due to the highly competitive nature of the airline industry, however, airlines frequently hired the lowest-bidding private security firms as a way to save money. Unfortunately, according to most experts, airline security pre-September 11 was exceedingly poor. For example, in undercover tests conducted before the attacks, airport screeners routinely failed to detect knives, guns, and other weapons carried by federal agents posing as passengers. Poor screener performance was the result of inadequate training, high job turnover, and low pay, according to the General Accounting Office, the investigative arm of Congress. The evident ease with which the September 11 hijackers carried out their plans was more than enough evidence for many critics that a change in aviation security was long overdue.

The newly established TSA has replaced private guards with better trained and more highly paid federal security agents at the nation's airports. The TSA is also replacing old screening technology with new bomb-screening systems. The agency's workforce has quickly grown to over seventy-three thousand employees, and the agency has plans to expand by taking over responsibility for security in every area of transportation.

Proponents of the new agency contend that the federal takeover has been beneficial. According to Air Transport Association spokesman Michael Wascom, "The system, in general, is in much better shape now. There was clearly a need for the government to assume responsibility for security, because airlines are not law-enforcement agencies." Proponents claim that despite having to complete the transition in a year's time, the agency has performed remarkably well. Memphis airport director Larry Cox says, "I've got to hand it to them; they've delivered on this." Cox, an early skeptic, was pleasantly surprised when the new, highly trained agents arrived at his airport in September 2002.

The TSA has its share of critics, however, most of whom claim that despite the amount of money now being thrown at the problem, airport security is no better today than it was before the September 11 attacks. Federal Aviation Administration whistle-blower Bogdan Dzakovic contends, "We could breach security 80 percent to 90 percent of the time with very little problem before September 11. Today, it's no different." Critics especially criticize the TSA's use of random passenger screening, claiming that the process is like looking for a needle in a haystack.

Most experts agree that September 11 demonstrated the need for greater airport security, but vociferous debate surrounds the government's response to that need. After viewing air travel as potentially fatal immediately after the attacks, now many Americans merely see airports as scenes of inconvenience and frustration. Waiting in long lines to be screened illicits groans in some, outrage in others. Syndicated columnist Don Feder complains, "These senseless rituals do nothing to thwart terrorism, but much to aggravate already harassed travelers." He adds, "Flying is getting to be as much fun as a root canal without Novocaine." The authors in the following chapter debate other responses to terrorism, such as waging war and restricting immigration. As the government's effort to improve airport security illustrates, responses to terrorist threats generate much controversy.

> "In combating international terrorism, the United States government is doing one of the few things that it has a clear and legitimate power to do."

The United States Should Wage War to Fight Terrorism

Stephen Cox

Stephen Cox maintains in the following viewpoint that killing terrorists and going to war with the states that sponsor them is the best way to respond to terrorism. He argues that pacifists hold a distorted view of the world, believing that if the United States stopped committing violence against individuals and nations, peace would naturally follow. On the contrary, he asserts, there will always be terrorists committed to harming America, and ignoring them will only encourage more acts of terrorism. Cox is a professor of literature at the University of California, San Diego.

As you read, consider the following questions:

1. How does Cox characterize the New Jerusalem?
2. How does the author use the movie *The Wizard of Oz* to support his argument that terrorist Osama bin Laden ought to be killed?
3. According to Cox, what are three ways to defeat terrorism?

Stephen Cox, "No Time for Fantasy," *Liberty*, vol. 15, December 2001, pp. 27–30, 61. Copyright © 2001 by Liberty Publishing. Reproduced by permission.

At the climax of the last book of the Bible, the book of Revelation, St. John presents his vision of the end of history:

> And I John saw the holy city, new Jerusalem, coming down from God out of heaven, prepared as a bride adorned for her husband. And I heard a great voice out of heaven saying, Behold, the tabernacle of God is with men . . . and God shall wipe away all tears from their eyes; and there shall be no more death, neither sorrow, nor crying, neither shall there be any more pain; for the former things are passed away.

For two thousand years, this vision has inspired the devout and amused the skeptical. But no one, until now, ever thought that the event had already taken place.

The New Jerusalem

No one, until now, ever thought that he was actually living in a world like the New Jerusalem, where pain and sorrow and death had become, well, obsolete. Only in the aftermath of the apocalyptic destruction of the World Trade Center [as a result of the September 11, 2001, terrorist attacks] has this mighty truth dawned upon the consciousness of a minority—but a significant minority—of Western intellectuals.

To these people (are you one of them?), the way to deal with the atrocity of September 11 is, basically, to ignore it. Yes, they admit that it happened. It was "shocking." It was "horrifying." They "grieve for the victims." But for them, terrorism still has an air of unreality. They see no necessity for the United States to engage in military retaliation. Quite the contrary. They believe that the terrorists will stop, if the United States does. They believe that America's enemies have good reasons for their enmity, and that it is up to America, therefore, to "end the cycle of violence." That means dropping the arrogant assumption that we have the right to punish foreign nations for the ("alleged") misdeeds of their residents. If we want to end terrorist attacks, we should look "beyond the horror of September 11" and think about how we can find nonviolent solutions to international problems.

Sounds good, doesn't it? Certainly it sounds good to the "signers and j'iners," the people who busy themselves sending out petitions for "justice, not revenge" and other self-evidently worthy causes. When they speak of peace and reason and cooperation, their satisfaction—indeed their self-satisfaction—always appears complete. Eloquent about the risks of war, they seem certain that nothing in their own proposals could possibly entail a risk. They appear certain, in other words, that they are already living in the New Jerusalem, in that blessed place where morality and practicality are, at last, one and the same, that place where there is no longer any necessity for death, neither sorrow, nor crying. To inhabit that risk-free world, all we need to do is to live, as St. John puts it, "in the Spirit."

It's interesting that nobody except Americans ever seems to reason in this way. Sure, there are zealots and thugs and morons all over the world who are willing to riot for "peace" at a moment's notice, but they know that the peace they seek can only be purchased at the price of destruction, the destruction not just of America's foreign alliances, military bases, and so forth, but also of American capitalism and any other identifiably American aspect of world culture. It's only Americans who get so carried away by evangelical beliefs as to imagine, not merely that everyone ought to be traveling toward that City on the Hill, but that everyone ought to act as if the journey had actually been completed.

Anti-Anti-Terrorist Bunk

I'm as vulnerable to the evangelical spirit as any other American. I always want to believe that we are half a mile from the New Jerusalem, and getting there fast. I have very strong isolationist and peace-freak proclivities. Nevertheless, even I know that the anti-anti-terrorist attitude is bunk. At best, it expresses a true idealism about peace and justice. At worst, it expresses a cruel disregard for reality.

This disregard achieves fantastic proportions in the idea that, pending judicial proceedings, no one should be "punished" for the September 11 atrocity. After all, it is said, we haven't seen all the evidence against [terrorist] Osama bin Laden. He may be guilty of nothing more than *saying* that he wants to have us all killed, riling up a few mobs here and there, running a few boot camps for weekend warriors, and, from time to time, blowing up a ship or an embassy somewhere. In sum, he may be little more than an "ideological role model" for the people who are trying to kill us.

Yes, I can see it now: Dorothy and her friends are walking along through Oz when, suddenly, the flying monkeys descend, abducting the girl and leaving her friends for dead. Well, who really knows who was responsible? True, the Wicked Witch showed up before, and made some threats—but maybe she was joking. Maybe she was just carried away by her own rhetoric. And, true, the flying monkeys are known to be allied with her—but maybe she didn't actually direct their attack. Remember, we have only the word of the Wizard that she is the focus of evil, and the Wizard has been known to lie. Clearly, no water should be poured on the Witch until she is arrested and tried at The Hague.

Sorry. She's a wicked witch, and she has to be killed. That will discourage the other wicked witches. And you can see what miraculous effects this kind of thing can have on a gang of flying monkeys. Once she was dead, all they could think of to say was, "Hail, Dorothy!" . . .

Three Things That Defeat Terrorism

So where do we go from here? There are three things that are capable of defeating terrorism.

The first, and potentially the most conclusive, is boredom. The terrorist movements of the late 19th century eventually fizzled out—partly, it seems, because the terrorists got bored with plotting to assassinate people. Some of them changed their political tactics; others, it seems, just grew up. Unfortunately, however, some of them kept at it, like the terrorists who started World War I; and it will never be known how many would have institutionalized themselves permanently, like the Irish Republican Army, if they had not been the targets of repressive measures.

The second means of defeating terrorism is, therefore, direct repression of the terrorists. Every dead terrorist is a terrorist who will never commit another act of terror. Sorry, peace dude: Violence often works. As to the idea that repression "creates martyrs," "sows dragon's teeth," "fuels more rage," and so forth . . . sometimes it does, but in this case, who cares? Maybe Osama bin Laden's untimely death will be avenged by a bunch of yahoos who decide to blow up the World Trade Center. Oops! That already happened. The terrorists were already fueled with enough rage to do that. Do you think that if we don't pursue bin Laden, they're going to say to themselves, "Oh, I guess we shouldn't blow up the Chrysler Building, after all." I don't think so. But if America's war on bin Laden is successful, some of them will say (to themselves), "Dude! That coulda been me. I think I'm gonna go back to Florida State and pick up that degree in computer science."

Living Lives of Fear and Loss

To back away from this war would be to live the rest of our lives, not just a few years, with skyscrapers and bridges exploding, people dying by terrorist bombs, chemical attacks, and the successive devices of sharp and ruthless minds, to live out our futures with our liberties shrinking as our losses and fears expand.

Scott Simon, *Friends Journal*, December 2001.

The third means is an attack on terrorist states. That's the approach that President Ronald Reagan took when he bombed Libya in 1986. Until then, Libya was a focus of terrorist activity. Now it's not. Why? We repressed Libya. We shouldn't be under any illusions about terrorism being a strictly spontaneous overflow of powerful feeling. Abou ben Adhem, age 18, native of Taliban City, Talibanistan, may be as mad as hell about America's squishing of his hero, Osama bin Laden, but he will probably be in no position to avenge the death, so long as he's unable to locate people who are well-organized and well-funded enough to help him. The trouble starts when he hooks up with some government-protected agency that gives him money and sanctuary and all the other stuff he needs to live as a professional terrorist with some prospect of a dramatic success. That's why America should do what it can to put terrorist states out of business.

Now, it's obvious, simply from the fact that we do *not* live in the New Jerusalem, that we have no guarantee that any of these three means of ending terrorism will totally succeed. There's no guarantee of total success in anything. But there are guarantees of failure. "Mr. bin Laden, we're really upset with you. We're going to investigate this situation, and if we find evidence that will stand up in court, we are going to insist that the government of Afghanistan extradite you to New York, where you will be given a fair trial and be either convicted or acquitted. As to force and coercion, we're not going to stoop to your level. Meanwhile, we're going to appoint a committee, headed by the Reverend Jesse Jackson, to review the question of Why People Who Hate Capitalism and Liberalism Also Hate America." That's what I'd call a guarantee of practical failure.

The Moral View

But let's take a strictly moral view of the situation. There are very few people, even radical libertarians, who would deny that the American government has a duty to pursue and punish any gang of Americans who murder 6,000 people for the purpose of emphasizing their own religious views. The legitimate purpose of the state, if any, is the protection of liberty and property. But if the state has the duty to go after a gang of Americans, is there any moral reason why it can't go after a gang of non-Americans who do the same thing? What? Does morality change at the border? Is there some reason to believe that the border of Afghanistan is more sacred than life, liberty, and property?

No, what's wrong with war is the prospect of people being shot, bombed, crushed, crippled, burned alive. That's why war is bad—not because it takes place on somebody else's soil, instead of our own. The war that America is in right now began on America's soil on September 11, 2001. It will continue on America's soil, indeed it will escalate, until (1) the terrorists get bored; (2) we get to the terrorists and kill them; (3) we take action against the states that support them and either neutralize or kill them, too. The first option is, unluckily, outside our power to implement. The second and third options seem to lie within our power.

Isn't it remarkable? In combating international terrorism, the United States government is doing one of the few things that it has a clear and legitimate power to do. And that's precisely what critics of the anti-terrorist campaign don't want it to do. They are good people, many of them. Their critiques of government, in other contexts, have often been extremely valuable. Now, however, they are doing little more than identifying themselves as politically irrelevant, and that is a shame and a loss.

There's another passage of Bible prophecy that speaks of this. It's in the sixth chapter of Jeremiah, and it's much more realistic than the Bible passage with which I started. Speaking of certain intellectuals of his time, Jeremiah says, "They have healed also the hurt of my people slightly, saying, Peace, peace: when there is no peace."

"[Military action] is likely to lead to more terrorism rather than less, and to decrease security rather than rebuilding it."

The United States Should Not Wage War to Fight Terrorism

Stephen G. Cary

In the following viewpoint Stephen G. Cary contends that going to war to fight terrorism will lead to more terrorism and decrease America's security. According to Cary, retaliation invites counterretaliation and increases the anger that many nations harbor toward the United States. Instead of going to war, Cary advocates more cooperation with the international community and a deeper examination of America's foreign policy. Cary, who died in 2002 shortly after writing this article, was a member and former head of the Germantown Friends Meeting in Philadelphia, Pennsylvania; a retired vice president of Haverford College; and had a long association with the American Friends Service Committee, a Quaker organization dedicated to social justice and peace.

As you read, consider the following questions:

1. In Cary's opinion, what has led the American people to endorse military action in response to the September 11, 2001, terrorist attacks?
2. What are the "beams in American eyes," according to the author?
3. What evidence of American arrogance does the author list?

Stephen G. Cary, "A Response to September Eleventh," *Friends Journal*, vol. 48, March 2002, pp. 8–11.

As a Quaker, a pacifist, and one of the 9 percent of U.S. citizens who dissent from our country's current response to the [September 11, 2001, terrorist attacks on the United States], many friends belonging to the 91 percent majority have asked me to explain my position. Piecemeal answers are time-consuming and unsatisfactory, so I have drafted this fuller statement that I can share with all interested.

Responding to Tragedy

It goes without saying that I share the view of all in the U.S. that what happened in New York and Washington was an unspeakable crime. I, too, want the perpetrators identified and brought to trial—preferably under international auspices. Those are givens.

There are two roots to our national anguish, either painful in itself, but together responsible for causing a level of shock as deep or deeper than Pearl Harbor. The first is our sadness over the terrible loss of lives and the pain we feel for those whose days will never be the same. The second is the harsh recognition of a new national vulnerability. For 300 years we have been secure behind our oceans. For 300 years we have been in control of our fate. The coming of the atomic and missile age actually ended that happy state of affairs a half-century ago but did not seize the nation until September 11, when it came like a bombshell. Citizens of the U.S. knew then that our world would never be the same. It was a stunning shock.

The question we face now is how to respond to this new reality, and this is where the 91 percent and the 9 percent part company. How do we differ? As I understand it, the 91 percent, under the president's leadership, hopes to regain control and restore at least a measure of invulnerability by building alliances, tracking down evildoers, and military action. In his words, "It is America's mission to rid the world of evil. We must root out the terrorists and stamp out terrorism, and we will do so." It is a new kind of war, against civilian populations, and not fought by opposing armies. Our military response will be measured, designed to flush the guilty from their hiding places and punishing enough to persuade those who harbor them to turn them over. The war's end is indefinite, but it will be long and will continue until the threat of terrorism is eliminated. The U.S. will stay the course. Justice will prevail.

The people of the U.S., traumatized by events, find comfort in a new national unity, based on a fervent patriotism that finds expressions in showing the flag, singing "God Bless America," arranging for 40 million children to simultaneously recite the pledge of allegiance, and congratulating ourselves on our role as the champions of justice and the torchbearers of freedom. This outpouring is reinforced by the full weight of the government, the media, and the entertainment, sports, and corporate communities, and leads to unquestioned backing of the bombing of Afghanistan as the opening phase of the new war.

A Dangerous State of Affairs

There is a need for comfort in trying times. The decline in partisan bickering and the coming together of our diverse society are welcome. But acquiescence has a downside in the present crisis because it silences dissent and the serious discussion of alternative policy directions. From my perspective, this is a dangerous state of affairs because the path down which we are going is likely to lead to more terrorism rather than less, and to decrease security rather than rebuilding it.

Why? First, because retaliation, whether identified as "punishment" or "justice," does not teach the enemy a lesson or lead it to change its ways. Retaliation stiffens, angers, and invites counterretaliation. If we have not learned that over the last half-century in the Middle East and Northern Ireland conflicts—to name just two of many settings where the tit-for-tat game has been on daily display—I don't know where we've been. Retaliation as a way to prevail against an enemy has, short of annihilation, been a failure. Has any benefit really accrued from the daily bombing of dirt-poor, starving, and chaotic Afghanistan? Has this really reduced the threat of terrorism?

Second, we will likely see more terrorism because our bombing will increase alienation, and in many countries, especially throughout the Arab world, add to hatred. It is already doing so. Polls taken in Turkey and Pakistan have shown that a shocking 80 percent of Turks and a majority of Pakistanis oppose our bombing, and a dangerous number even supports bin Laden. It is just this hatred that produces the fetid soil from which the terror masters recruit their troops. (Compare: the rise of Hitler in an embittered Germany in the wake of a vindictive Versailles.) If we succeed in capturing bin Laden, there will be plenty of others prepared to take his place. Increasing hatred assures more terrorism. In sum, I believe the president's "crusade against wickedness" will fail.

Motes and Beams

What is my alternative? How seriously should I take the instructions for dealing with enemies given to me by Jesus, whom I claim to be my guide, my brother, and my master? There is no doubt about where he stood. He made it clear in the greatest of his sermons when he preached to the multitude from a mountaintop: "And why beholdest thou the mote that is in thy brother's eye, but considerest not the beam that is in thine own eye? . . . Thou hypocrite, first cast out the beam out of thine own eye; and then shalt thou see clearly to cast out the mote out of thy brother's eye." (Matt. 7:3–5)

War Is Terrorism

We need new ways of thinking. A $300 billion military budget has not given us security. Military bases all over the world, our warships on every ocean, have not given us security. . . . We need to decide that we will not go to war, whatever reason is conjured up by the politicians or the media, because war in our time is always indiscriminate, a war against innocents, a war against children. War is terrorism, magnified a hundred times.

Howard Zinn, *Progressive Populist*, October 15, 2001.

Reflecting on these words is not a popular exercise for Christians these days. Brushing them aside has been made easier, first, by the efforts of theologians who for 2,000 years have found them too uncompromising and have looked for ways to temper them without repudiating their preacher; and, second, by claiming that Osama bin Laden is a new and more terrible devil than the world has ever known, who must be dealt with differently.

Neither of these rationalizations is satisfying. I believe Jesus meant what he said because his words are no less than a faithful reflection of the vibrant witness of his own life. Nor can I accept the convenient bin Laden argument. Jesus' world was at least as brutal as our own, his country under military occupation, and its terrorist differing from ours in name only. His name was Herod and his al-Qaida [network] was his army.

These reflections have made me think about motes and beams. What are the beams in our American eyes that make people hate us? And if we can remove them won't that lessen hatred and reduce terrorism? Human beings do not fly civilian airplanes into buildings to kill 3,000 innocent people without harboring a depth of anger that makes them easy targets for a bin Laden to persuade them that in doing so they will become God's martyrs. We in the U.S. live with illusion if we do not recognize that there are millions, especially in the Arab and Muslim worlds, who harbor this kind of feeling toward us. Doesn't it make sense in such a circumstance to ask what options are open to us to ease this dangerous situation? A few voices are doing so, but I have yet to hear a single word on the subject from any government source. Indeed, to the contrary, President George W. Bush has been widely quoted as saying that he, "like most Americans, is amazed that people would hate us because I know how good we are." With all due respect, I am appalled at the shallowness of such a comment from the most powerful man in the world.

I think there are things that we can do that would point us in a new and more hopeful direction. I identify them in what follows in the hope that they will provoke thought:

Aid to Others

We need to take a fresh look at our outreach to the world's poor, its hungry, its oppressed and illiterate, its sick, its millions of refugees. We think of ourselves as generous and caring. The reality is otherwise. The U.S. is by far the most miserly of all the world's industrialized nations in the percentage of resources it allocates to nonmilitary assistance to the underdeveloped world. I think we should be troubled when we glance at our current budget: $340 billion for the power to kill; $6 billion for power to lift the quality of life of the poor and dispossessed, on whose succor peace ultimately depends.

World Arms Trade

Shouldn't we reexamine our role as the largest player in the worldwide trade in arms? We justify it on the grounds that it helps democratic allies defend themselves against aggressor nations, but often they are dispersed on the basis of two other criteria, (1) the ability to pay, or (2) the recipient's qualification as the enemy of our enemy and therefore entitled to our weapons. It is this armament that frequently ends up in the hands of tyrants and is used to oppress their people or attack their neighbors. A poignant current example: Afghanistan, where we armed the Taliban because they were fighting the Russians, but who then used our largess to seize power, with tragic results. The arms trade is great for Lockheed, but a curse to the world, and a source of slaughter from which hatred is spawned.

Sanctions against Iraq

Shouldn't we be concerned about the 5,000–6,000 Iraqi children who die every month because of U.S.-supported sanctions? Aren't these lives just as precious as those so wantonly destroyed on September 11? The sanctions are of course aimed at Saddam Hussein, but after years they have left him stronger than ever, and they are being ignored by many nations, including close allies. What purpose are they serving to justify the added burden of hatred they provoke?

The Role of the CIA

Whatever it may have accomplished that we don't know about, what we do know should raise the grave concern of all in the U.S. Particularly egregious has been its role in arranging coups that overthrow governments we don't like, even popularly elected ones. The list is long—Guatemala, Chile, Iran, Cambodia, to name several. Do we in the U.S. have any awareness of the millions of human beings slaughtered by the regimes we installed in their place or opened the way for? I have personally seen the tragedies we wrought in three of those examples: Chile, Guatemala, and Cambodia—and it is an appalling record. Our readiness to interfere in the internal affairs of other nations poisons our image, especially when others see the firestorm that erupts here when foreigners mess into our affairs, even when through relatively innocuous illegal contributions to our political campaigns.

U.S. Policies in the Middle East

This is the most sensitive and difficult concern for me to raise, but because it is probably the most important source of hatred of the U.S. throughout the Muslim world, where the greatest threat of terrorism is centered, I have to speak to it despite my full support of an independent Israel. The problem is the perceived 50-year imbalance in our stance in the Israeli-Palestinian conflict.

I speak to this issue on the basis of three visits to the West Bank and Gaza over the last 20 years, and six weeks living in Jerusalem, with instructions to focus on meeting with Likud officials to better understand their point of view. There are a number of factors that underlie Arab anger:

(a) The harshness of Palestinian life under a half-century of brutal Israeli military occupation—brutal not because it is Israeli, but because any occupation in a hostile environment is brutal. Neither people in the U.S. nor, indeed, many Israelis, have any idea of what the daily life of a Palestinian is like, and has been for 50 years: arbitrary cutting off of livelihoods; daily encounters with checkpoints often involving long delays; land seizures; unfair allotment of water; summary trials in military courts; sudden shutting down of schools and colleges; blowing up of homes; thousands trapped in squalid refugee camps since 1948. I wish U.S. and Israeli policymakers could spend two weeks living with a Palestinian family; they might better understand the rock throwers.

(b) Massive military aid to Israel. This is justified as necessary to assure its security in a hostile environment, but U.S. weapons, from heavy tanks to helicopter gunships, kill Palestinians at a ten-to-one rate and give Israel overwhelming superiority in the brutal game of mutual retaliation. This adds to Arab anger and robs us of the neutrality required of a broker in peace negotiations.

(c) The Israeli settlement program. Deliberately designed to honeycomb the West Bank to make a potential Palestinian state geographically impossible, and involving the seizure of large blocks of land without warning or compensation and the eviction of all who live on it, the program has always been a massive obstacle to any meaningful peace settlement. Yet for over 30 years the U.S. has made only the most modest protests and has made it financially possible by large grants of nonmilitary aid that have served annually to free Israeli funds for its construction program. Some years ago, I was sitting in the office of Mayor Freij of Bethlehem when he pointed across a valley at a settlement under construction and said, "Mr. Cary, I have friends whose family has lived on that land for 700 years. They were just told to get out. We could do nothing. Do you blame us for being angry? I can promise you one thing: the Israelis will never know peace until this sort of injustice is ended. You Americans could have stopped this program, but you weren't interested in doing so."

(d) Highways crisscross the West Bank to assure easy passage between Jerusalem and the settlements. Cars with Israeli license plates can reach most of their destinations in 20 to 40 minutes, while Palestinian cars take several hours because of holdups at military checkpoints.

(e) I've mentioned water. I do so again to underline that because it is in such short supply throughout the region, its allocation is a major issue. Israel controls all water resources, and in the eyes of Palestinians, its allocation is so unfair that it is a source of bitterness, of which they are reminded daily.

(f) Terror. We rightly condemn and give full press coverage to Palestinian terror—the blowing up of Israeli buses and the tossing of bombs into marketplaces— but where has been the outrage, or even press mention, of the Israeli practice over many years of forcibly removing Palestinian families from their homes and bulldozing or dynamiting them because a relative has been accused of being a terrorist? Isn't this cruel retaliation against innocent people also terrorism?

Or, to cite a more recent, specific example of terrorism:

the assassination of Israeli Tourism Minister Rehavan Zeevi. You will remember that a few months before his killing the Israelis assassinated two radical Palestinians (in what they labeled "preemptive strikes") by blowing up their cars from helicopter gun ships (U.S. provided). The Palestinian response: nothing—not, alas, by choice, but because they had nothing to respond with. In contrast, the Israeli response to the Zeevi killing: heavy tanks (U.S. provided) sent into ten Palestinian towns, at the cost of 25 Palestinian lives—all in territory turned over, at least in theory, to the Palestinian Authority. I don't justify assassination under any circumstances, but there's hardly been a clearer example of the imbalance of power (courtesy of the U.S.) that is such a bitter source of Arab anger.

The Arrogance of Power

Throughout history great powers and empires have always been tempted to go it alone, to pursue their own interests without regard for the interests of others. England was the victim of this mindset throughout the 19th century. In the 21st, are the immense wealth and power of the United States taking us down this road? Some troubling evidence:

(a) Our stance toward the United Nations. We call on it when it suits our purposes, but ignore or denounce it when it doesn't. We don't pay the dues we solemnly committed ourselves to pay because some things about the organization displease us. This petty behavior badly hurts our image around the world.

(b) We walk away from treaties we signed and ratified, but which we no longer want to be bound by. A current example is the Anti-Ballistic Missile Treaty, the cornerstone of arms control for the past 20 years.

(c) Ignoring, vetoing, or reneging on a whole range of negotiated agreements that enjoy overwhelming support of the world community, but which we don't like because they may limit our freedom of action. Examples: the Kyoto agreements on global warming, the Nuclear Test Ban Treaty, the elimination of land mines, the Law of the Seas agreement, the establishment of an international war crimes court, and the regulation of international trade in small arms.

The Community of Nations

Wouldn't a more generous, cooperative role in the community of nations, instead of readiness to go it alone because we are the superpower that nobody can challenge, help to change our image and lessen anti-Americanism around the world?

Earlier, I spoke of identifying and bringing to trial the perpetrators of September 11 as "a given," but I haven't mentioned the subject since. It is still a given, but it has a different priority with me than with the nation's 91 percent.

Blasting Osama bin Laden and his lieutenants from their caves or killing them on the run will satisfy the widespread desire for vengeance, but its price is too high and its contribution to easing the threat of terrorism too low. Destruction of a starving country and blowing up Red Cross relief depots, hospitals, and residential areas—however unintentionally—only add to the anger that is the root cause of terrorism.

I give priority to pursuing other avenues that promise to improve the international climate to the point where diplomatic and legal initiatives can produce the culprits for trial and punishment. Biding our time will prove less costly than dropping megaton bombs.

I have wanted to give some sort of answer to the many friends who are troubled by bombing and retaliation, but ask, often plaintively, "But what else can we do?" My suggestions are of things that in the long run would seem to me to be more likely to free us from terrorism and restore security than rooting out bin Laden by twisting arms to build temporary military alliances, meeting violence with violence, and bombing poor countries.

Making the Case for Peace

In making my case, however, I have two problems. The first is how to speak forcefully on so many issues without coming across as anti-American and/or anti-Israel perceptions bound to produce more heat than light. It's also frustrating because I am as devoted to our nation as any flag-waver. My aim—and my definition of patriotism—is to help a great country become greater, and more worthy of its dreams.

My second problem is the impression I may convey that the United States is the only one responsible for bringing terror on itself, which is patently not the case. We are one player among many. Other countries, including nations in the Arab world, are guilty of sins of omission and commission that have contributed to the present poisoned atmosphere, and which must be addressed. My position is only that we are complicit, and should undertake our response to September 11 where it is easiest and most important to do so—where our own house is out of order and where we can ourselves do things that will contribute to easing the world's sickness.

We must move beyond the naive but satisfying illusion that "we" are good and "they" are evil—that the devil always lives somewhere else: now in Berlin and Tokyo; now in Moscow, Hanoi, and Beijing; now on to Belgrade and Kabul; but never in Washington. The devil lives in the hearts of all of God's children, and until we take responsibility to try to lift up that which is good in us and cast out that which is bad, the scourge of terrorism will continue to torment us.

"Winning [the war against terrorism] may require the use of preemptive force against terrorist forces as well as against the states that harbor them."

Preemptive Strikes Are a Legitimate Option for Fighting Terrorism

Michael J. Glennon

According to Michael J. Glennon in the following viewpoint, careful use of preemptive strikes against terrorists and the nations that harbor them is a legitimate method for protecting national security. He argues against claims that preemptive strikes run counter to international laws forbidding the use of force except in self-defense. In fact, he points out, such laws are archaic, as evidenced by the majority of United Nations members who have used preemptive strikes. Michael J. Glennon is a fellow at the Woodrow Wilson International Center for Scholars in Washington, D.C.; professor of law at the University of California, Davis, Law School; and author of *Limits of Law, Prerogatives of Power: Interventionism After Kosovo.*

As you read, consider the following questions:
1. What does Article 51 of the UN Charter state, as cited by Glennon?
2. In what five ways have security needs changed since 1945, in the author's opinion?

The Bush Doctrine, as promulgated by President Bush following the September 11, 2001, [terrorist attacks on America] contemplates preemptive use of force against terrorists as well as the states that harbor them. If the United Nations Charter is to be believed, however, carrying out that doctrine would be unlawful: The Charter permits use of force by states only in response to an armed attack. In 1945, when the Charter was framed, this prohibition against anticipatory self-defense may have seemed realistic. Today, it is not. Indeed, it is no longer binding law.

War and Self-Defense

Since time immemorial, the use of force has been permitted in self-defense in the international as well as all domestic legal systems, and for much the same reason: With states as with individuals, the most elemental right is survival. So powerful has been its claim that the right of self-defense was considered implicit in earlier treaties limiting use of force by states; the Kellogg-Briand Peace Pact of 1928, like the 1919 Covenant of the League of Nations, made no mention of it.

In 1945, the right was made explicit. Article 51 of the United Nations Charter states expressly: "Nothing in the present Charter shall impair the inherent right of individual or collective self-defense if an armed attack occurs against a Member of the United Nations. . . ." Self-defense thus emerged as the sole purpose under the Charter for which states may use force without Security Council approval.

While the Charter professes not to "impair" the inherent right to self-defense, it does precisely that. Prior to 1945, states used defensive force *before* an attack had occurred, to *forestall* an attack. The plain language of Article 51 permits defensive use of force only *if* an armed attack occurs. If none has occurred, defensive force—"anticipatory self-defense"— is not permitted.

This new impairment of the right of self-defense was widely seen as sensible when the Charter was adopted. States had often used the claim of self-defense as a pretext for aggression. (The Nazi defendants at Nuremberg argued that Germany had attacked the Soviet Union, Norway, and Denmark in self-defense, fearing that Germany was about to be attacked.) If profligate use of force was ever to be reined in, narrower limits had to be imposed. And those limits had to be set out with a bright line; qualifying defensive rights with words like "reasonable," "imminent," or even "necessary" would leave states too much discretion and too much room for abuse. The occurrence of an actual armed attack was thus set up as an essential predicate for the use of force. The new requirement narrowed significantly the circumstances in which force could be used. And it set out a readily identifiable and, it was thought, objectively verifiable event to trigger defensive rights. Phony defensive justifications would be less plausible and war would be less frequent, thereby vindicating the first great purpose of the Charter—"to maintain international peace and security."

The impairment was realistic, it was further thought, because the need for anticipatory defense would diminish. The reason was that the UN Security Council would pick up where individual states were now compelled by the Charter to leave off. The Council, to be equipped with its own standing or standby forces, was authorized to use force in response to any "threat to the peace"—authority far broader than that accorded individual states. Coupled with the requirement that states report to the Security Council when using defensive force, this new institution—this "constabulary power before which barbaric and atavistic forces will stand in awe," as [British Prime Minister Winston] Churchill described it—would make anticipatory self-help a thing of the past.

All know that it didn't work out that way. Throughout the Cold War the Security Council deadlocked repeatedly on security issues. States never gave the Council the peace enforcement troops contemplated by the Charter's framers. The Council authorized (rather than used) force only haphazardly "to maintain or restore international peace and security." And, as discussed later, states continued to use force often, obviously not in response to armed attacks.

Preemptive Precedents

Still, like most states, the United States never formally claimed a right to anticipatory self-defense—i.e., to use armed force absent an armed attack, so as to prevent one from occurring. During the 1962 Cuban Missile Crisis, the United States declined to rely upon Article 51, claiming instead that the "quarantine" of Cuba was authorized by the Organization of American States (and implicitly by the Security Council). When Israel seemed to assert a right to use defensive force to prevent an imminent Arab attack in June 1967, and even when Israel squarely claimed that right in attacking an Iraqi nuclear reactor in 1981, the United States steered clear of the issue of anticipatory self-defense. In 1986, however, the United States finally did claim the right to use "preemptive" force against Libya following the bombing of a Berlin night club that killed two Americans.

This last incident is worth considering closely: The Libyan bombing highlights the doctrinal confusion surrounding self-defense and also marks a proverbial "paradigm shift" in American thinking on the question. Why insist upon an actual armed attack as a precondition for the use of force? The axiomatic answer, under long-standing dogma, is of course that force is necessary to protect against the attack. But by acknowledging that its use of force against Libya was preemptive, the United States in effect moved beyond the conventional justification. The Berlin bombing was obviously over and finished; no use of force was, or conceivably could have been, instrumental in "defending" Americans killed at the Berlin club. The United States was not, in this sense, responding *defensively*. It was engaged in a forward-looking action, an action directed at future, not past, attacks on Americans. Its use of force against Libya was triggered by the Berlin attack only in the sense that that attack was *evidence of the threat of future attacks*. Evidence of Libyan capabilities and intentions sufficient to warrant preemptive force might well have taken (and, in fact, also did take) the form of intelligence reports. From a purely epistemological standpoint, no actual armed attack was necessary.

Although the United States did not spell out its thinking this explicitly, in later incidents it acted on precisely this future-looking rationale. True, the United States was in each instance able to argue that actual armed attacks had occurred. But in each of those subsequent incidents, the

United States was *responding to evidence of future intent and capability*, not defending against past action. Its objective was to avert future attacks through preemption and deterrence.

This Nation Will Act

For much of the last century, America's defense relied on the cold war doctrines of deterrence and containment. In some cases, those strategies still apply, but new threats also require new thinking. Deterrence—the promise of massive retaliation against nations—means nothing against shadowy terrorist networks with no nation or citizens to defend. Containment is not possible when unbalanced dictators with weapons of mass destruction can deliver those weapons on missiles or secretly provide them to terrorist allies. We cannot defend America and our friends by hoping for the best. We cannot put our faith in the word of tyrants who solemnly sign nonproliferation treaties and then systemically break them. If we wait for threats to fully materialize, we will have waited too long.

Homeland defense and missile defense are part of stronger security; they're essential priorities for America. Yet, the war on terror will not be won on the defensive. We must take the battle to the enemy, disrupt his plans, and confront the worst threats before they emerge. In the world we have entered, the only path to safety is the path of action, and this Nation will act. . . .

Our security will require all Americans to be forward-looking and resolute, to be ready for preemptive action when necessary to defend our liberty and to defend our lives.

George W. Bush, Commencement Address at the U.S. Military Academy in West Point, New York, June 10, 2002.

In 1993, for example, the United States fired cruise missiles at the Iraqi intelligence headquarters in Baghdad following an alleged effort by Iraq to assassinate President George Bush. But the assassination attempt was long since over; the United States used force not to defend against illicit force already deployed, but to discourage such force from being deployed in the future. In 1998, the United States fired cruise missiles at a terrorist training camp in Afghanistan and a pharmaceutical plant in Sudan following attacks on U.S. embassies in Kenya and Tanzania. Again, the provocation had ended; in no way can the United States be seen as having defended itself against the specific armed attack to which its embassies had been subject.

Today's War on Terrorism

So, too, with the use of force against Afghanistan following September 11. The armed attack against the World Trade Center and the Pentagon was over, and no defensive action could have ameliorated its effects. The U.S. use of force was prompted by the threat of future attacks. And it was evidence of that threat—gleaned from multiple intelligence sources, not simply from the September 11 attack—to which the United States responded with its action against Afghanistan. That action could well have been warranted even if September 11 had never occurred. The problem lay in the future, not the past.

In each of these incidents, the United States justified its action under Article 51 of the Charter, claiming to be engaged in the *defensive* use of force. But in fact something different was going on. In each incident, the United States was—as it acknowledged forthrightly following the 1986 bombing of Libya—engaged in the use of *preemptive* force. The two are not the same. The justification for genuine defensive force was set forth by U.S. Secretary of State Daniel Webster in the famous *Caroline* case of 1837. To use it, he wrote, a state must "show a necessity of self-defense, instant, overwhelming, leaving no choice of means, and no moment of deliberation." (This formula continues to be widely cited by states, tribunals, and commentators as part and parcel of the law of the Charter.) Obviously, in none of the incidents canvassed above can the American use of force be said to meet the *Caroline* standard. None of the American armed responses needed to be, or was, instant. In each the United States deliberated for weeks or months before responding, carefully choosing its means. Those means were directed not at *defending against* an attack that had already begun, but at *preempting*, or *deterring*, an attack that *could* begin at some point in the future.

In fact, the United States had long ago accepted the logic of using armed force without waiting to be attacked. In the early 1960s, President John F. Kennedy seriously considered launching a preemptive strike against the People's Republic of China to prevent it from developing nuclear weapons. In 1994, President Bill Clinton contemplated a preemptive attack against North Korea for the same reason. During the Cold War, the United States retained the option of launching its nuclear weapons upon warning that a nuclear attack was about to occur—before the United States actually had been attacked—so as to protect command and control systems that were vulnerable to a Soviet first strike.

It thus came as no dramatic policy change when, in the Bush Doctrine, the United States publicly formalized its rejection of the armed attack requirement and officially announced its acceptance of preemption as a legitimate rationale for the use of force. "Every nation now knows," President George W. Bush said on December 11, "that we cannot accept—and we will not accept—states that harbor, finance, train, or equip the agents of terror."

Different Security Needs

That formalization was overdue. Twenty-first-century security needs are different from those imagined in San Francisco in 1945.

First, as noted above, the intended safeguard against unlawful threats of force—a vigilant and muscular Security Council—never materialized. Self-help is the only realistic alternative.

Second, modern methods of intelligence collection, such as satellite imagery and communications intercepts, now make it unnecessary to sit out an actual armed attack to await convincing proof of a state's hostile intent.

Third, with the advent of weapons of mass destruction and their availability to international terrorists, the first blow can be devastating—far more devastating than the pinprick attacks on which the old rules were premised.

Fourth, terrorist organizations "of global reach" were unknown when Article 51 was drafted. To flourish, they need to conduct training, raise money, and develop and stockpile weaponry—which in turn requires communications equipment, camps, technology, staffing, and offices. All this requires a sanctuary, which only states can provide—and which only states can take away.

Fifth, the danger of catalytic war erupting from the use of preemptive force has lessened with the end of the Cold War. It made sense to hew to Article 51 during the Cuban Missile Crisis, when two nuclear superpowers confronted each other toe-to-toe. It makes less sense today, when safe-haven states and terrorist organizations are not themselves possessed of preemptive capabilities.

Caveats

Still, it must be acknowledged that, at least in the short term, wider use of preemptive force could be destabilizing. The danger exists that some states threatened with preemptive action (consider India and Pakistan) will be all too ready to preempt probable preemptors. This is another variant of the quandary confronted when states, in taking steps to enhance their security, unintentionally threaten the security of adversaries—and thus find their own security diminished as adversaries take compensatory action.

But the way out of the dilemma, here as elsewhere, is not underreaction and concession. The way out lies in the adoption of prudent defensive strategies calculated to meet reasonably foreseeable security threats that pose a common danger. Such strategies generate community support and cause adversaries to adapt perceptions and, ultimately, to recalibrate their intentions and capabilities. That process can take time, during which the risk of greater systemic instability must be weighed against the risk of worldwide terrorist attacks of increased frequency and magnitude.

The greater danger is not long-term instability but the possibility that use of preemptive force could prove incomplete or ineffective. It is not always possible to locate all maleficent weapons or facilities, thereby posing the risk that some will survive a preemptive strike and be used in retaliation. Similarly, if a rogue state such as Iraq considers itself the likely target of preemptive force, its leaders may have an incentive to defend with weapons of mass destruction—weapons they would not otherwise use—in the belief that they have nothing to lose. A reliable assessment of likely costs is an essential precondition to any preemptive action.

These are the sorts of considerations that policymakers

must weigh in deciding whether to use preemptive force. Preemption obviously is a complement, not a stand-alone alternative, to non-coercive policy options. When available, those options normally are preferable. The point here is simply that preemption is a legitimate option, and that—the language of the Charter notwithstanding—preemption is lawful. States can no longer be said to regard the Charter's rules concerning anticipatory self-defense—or concerning the use of force in general, for that matter—as binding. The question—the sole question, in the consent-based international legal system—is whether states have in fact agreed to be bound by the Charter's use-of-force rules. If states had truly intended to make those rules obligatory, they would have made the cost of violation greater than the perceived benefits.

They have not. The Charter's use-of-force rules have been widely and regularly disregarded. Since 1945, two-thirds of the members of the United Nations—126 states out of 189—have fought 291 interstate conflicts in which over 22 million people have been killed. In every one of those conflicts, at least one belligerent necessarily violated the Charter. In most of those conflicts, most of the belligerents claimed to act in self-defense. States' earlier intent, expressed in words, has been superseded by their later intent, expressed in deeds.

Rather, therefore, than split legal hairs about whether a given use of force is an armed reprisal, intervention, armed attack, aggression, forcible countermeasure, or something else in international law's over-schematized catalogue of misdeeds, American policymakers are well advised to attend directly to protecting the safety and well-being of the American people. For fifty years, despite repeated efforts, the international community has been unable to agree on when the use of force is lawful and when it is not. There will be plenty of time to resume that discussion when the war on terrorism is won. If the "barbaric and atavistic" forces succeed, however, there will be no point in any such discussion, for the law of the jungle will prevail. Completing that victory is the task at hand. And winning may require the use of preemptive force against terrorist forces as well as against the states that harbor them.

*"[The policy of using preemptive strikes]
is a doctrine without limits, without
accountability, . . . without any convincing
demonstration of practical necessity."*

Preemptive Strikes Are Immoral and Unnecessary

Richard Falk

In the following viewpoint Richard Falk argues against the use of preemptive strikes against nations that harbor terrorists. The preemptive strike strategy, advocated by President George W. Bush and often referred to as "The Bush Doctrine," runs counter to long-standing international rules prohibiting the use of international force unless for self-defense, he asserts. Falk maintains that the United States is abandoning its successful deterrence and containment strategies in order to dispossess foreign powers of any weapons that might threaten America's dominance. According to Falk, the best way to improve America's security is to work with the global community for the establishment of peace. Falk is currently Visiting Distinguished Professor at the University of California, Santa Barbara.

As you read, consider the following questions:

1. What is the core idea of the United Nations Charter, according to Falk?
2. In the author's opinion, what fears in Washington have prompted the adoption of a preemptive strike strategy?
3. What does Falk see as the problem with America occupying the moral high ground with respect to other nations?

Richard Falk, "The New Bush Doctrine," *The Nation*, vol. 275, July 15, 2002, p. 9.

President George W. Bush's June 2002 graduation address to the cadets at West Point has attracted attention mainly because it is the fullest articulation, so far, of the new strategic doctrine of pre-emption. The radical idea being touted by the White House and Pentagon is that the United States has the right to use military force against any state that is seen as hostile or makes moves to acquire weapons of mass destruction—nuclear, biological or chemical. The obvious initial test case for pre-emption is Iraq, whose government the United States is continually threatening to overthrow, either on the model of the displacement of the Taliban in Afghanistan or by some other method. Washington's war plans have evidently not been finalized, and whether the intimations of war—despite the numerous objections voiced by neighboring governments and European allies—are to be taken literally is still unclear.

Defying the UN Charter

What is certain, and scary, is the new approach to the use of international force beneath the banner of counterterrorism and in the domestic climate of fervent nationalism that has existed since [the September 11, 2001, terrorist attacks on America]. This new approach repudiates the core idea of the United Nations Charter (reinforced by decisions of the World Court in The Hague), which prohibits any use of international force that is not undertaken in self-defense after the occurrence of an armed attack across an international boundary or pursuant to a decision by the UN Security Council. When Iraq conquered and annexed Kuwait in 1990, Kuwait was legally entitled to act in self-defense to recover its territorial sovereignty even without any UN authorization. And the United States and others were able to join Kuwait in bolstering its prospects, thereby acting in what international lawyers call collective self-defense.

Back in 1956, when the American commitment to this Charter effort to limit the discretion of states to the extent possible was still strong, the U.S. government surprised its allies and adversaries by opposing the Suez war of Britain, France and Israel because it was a nondefensive use of force against Egypt, despite the provocations associated at the time with Nasser's anti-Israeli, anti-Western militancy. This legal commitment had evolved by stages in the period after World War I, and when the surviving leaders of Germany and Japan were prosecuted for war crimes [after World War II], "crimes against the peace" were declared to be even worse than atrocities committed in the course of the war. The task of the Charter was to give this concept as clear limits as possible.

Pre-emption, in contrast, validates striking first—not in a crisis, as was done by Israel with plausible, if not entirely convincing, justification in the 1967 war, when enemy Arab troops were massing on its borders after dismissing the UN war-preventing presence—but on the basis of shadowy intentions, alleged potential links to terrorist groups, supposed plans and projects to acquire weapons of mass destruction, and anticipations of possible future dangers. It is a doctrine without limits, without accountability to the UN or international law, without any dependence on a collective judgment of responsible governments and, what is worse, without any convincing demonstration of practical necessity.

Abandoning the Rules of Law

It is true that the reality of the mega-terrorist challenge requires some rethinking of the relevance of rules and restraints based on conflict in a world of territorial states. The most radical aspects of the Al Qaeda [terrorist network] challenge are a result of its nonterritorial, concealed organizational reality as a multistate network. Modern geopolitics was framed to cope with conflict, and relations among sovereign states; the capacity of a network with modest resources to attack and wage a devastating type of war against the most powerful state does require acknowledgment that postmodern geopolitics needs a different structure of security.

Postmodernity refers here to preoccupations that can no longer be reduced to territorial dimensions. This contrasts with "modernity," born internationally in 1648 at the Peace of Westphalia with the emergence of the secular sovereign state, and a world politics that could be understood by reference to territorial ambitions and defense. For [terrorist] Osama bin Laden, the focus has been on nonterritorial empowerment via mega-terrorism, with the vision of an Islamic umma replacing the modern, Western-inspired structure of distinct sovereign states. For George W. Bush, the emphasis has been on carrying the retaliatory war to the networked enemy concealed in some sixty countries, and on declaring war against all those nonstate forces around the world.

To respond to the threat of mega-terrorism does require some stretching of international law to accommodate the reasonable security needs of sovereign states. Prior cross-border military reactions to transnational terrorism over the years by the United States, India, Israel and others were generally tolerated by the UN and international public opinion because they seemed proportionate and necessary in relation to the threats posed, and the use of force relied upon was in its essence reactive, not anticipatory. International law was bent to serve these practical imperatives of security, but not broken. But the Bush doctrine of pre-emption goes much further, encroaching on highly dangerous terrain. It claims a right to abandon rules of restraint and of law patiently developed over the course of centuries, rules governing the use of force in relation to territorial states, not networks.

Deterrence and Containment

To propose abandoning the core legal restraint on international force in relations among states is to misread the challenge of September 11. It permits states to use force nondefensively against their enemies, thereby creating a terrible precedent. There is every reason to think that containment and deterrence remain effective ways to approach a state that threatens unwarranted expansion. There is no evidence to suggest that Iraq cannot be deterred, and its pattern of behavior in relation to its war against Iran in the 1980s, as well as its conquest and annexation of Kuwait in 1990, were based on a rational calculation of gains that, when proved incorrect, led to a reversal of policy. Brutal and oppressive as the regime in Iraq is, it was accepted until 1990 as a geopolitical ally of sorts. As a state, it acts and behaves normally, that is, by weighing benefits and costs. It is surrounded and threatened by superior force, and any attempt to lash out at neighbors or others would almost certainly result in its immediate and total destruction. There is no reason whatsoever to think that deterrence and containment would not succeed, even should Baghdad manage to acquire biological, chemical or nuclear weapons. Deterrence and containment succeeded in relation to the Soviet Union for more than four decades, under far more demanding circumstances.

What is at stake with pre-emption, as tied to the "axis of evil" imagery [George W. Bush has used to describe Iraq, Iran, and North Korea], is more hidden and sinister. What is feared in Washington, I think, is not aggressive moves by these countries but their acquisition of weapons of mass destruction that might give them a deterrent capability with respect to the United States and other nations. Since the end of the cold war the United States has enjoyed the luxury of being undeterred in world politics. It is this circumstance that makes Bush's "unilateralism" particularly disturbing to other countries, and it must be understood in relation to the moves of the Pentagon, contained in a report leaked in December 2001, to increase U.S. reliance on nuclear weapons in a variety of strategic circumstances. At West Point, Bush declared with moral fervor that "our enemies . . . have been caught seeking these terrible weapons." It never occurs to our leaders that these weapons are no less terrible when in the hands of the United States, especially when their use is explicitly contemplated as a sensible policy option. There is every reason for others to fear that when the United States is undeterred it will again become subject to "the Hiroshima temptation," in which it might threaten and use such weapons in the absence of any prospect of retaliation.

Hypocritical Hegemony

Bush goes further, combining empire with utopia, reminding his West Point audience that "the twentieth century ended with a single surviving model of human progress based on nonnegotiable demands of human dignity, the rule of law, limits on the power of the state, respect for women and private property, and free speech and equal justice and religious tolerance." The clear intention is to suggest that America is the embodiment of this model. And while Bush does concede that "America cannot impose this vision," he does propose that it "can support and reward governments that make the right choices for their own people," and presumably punish those that don't. Not only does the United States claim the right to global dominance but it also professes to have the final answers for societal well-being, seeming to forget its homeless, its crowded and expanding prisons, its urban blight and countless other domestic reminders that ours may not be the best of all possible worlds, and especially not for all possible peoples.

This vision of postmodern geopolitics is underwritten by a now-familiar strong message of evangelical moralism. Bush notes that "some worry that it is somehow undiplomatic or impolite to speak the language of right and wrong. I disagree," and adds that "moral truth is the same in every culture, in every time, and in every place." Such moral absolutism is then applied to the current global realities. Bush insists that "we are in a conflict between good and evil, and America will call evil by its name. By confronting evil and lawless regimes, we do not create a problem, we reveal a problem. And we will lead the world in opposing it." Aside from occupying the moral high ground, which exempts America from self-criticism or from addressing the grievances others have with respect to our policies, such sentiments imply a repudiation of dialogue and negotiation. As there can be no acceptable compromise with the forces of evil, there can be no reasonable restraint on the forces of good. We may lament fundamentalism in the Islamic world and decry the fulminations of Osama bin Laden, but what about our own?

America Is Not That Kind of Country

Unilateral preventive war is neither legitimate nor moral. It is illegitimate and immoral. For more than 200 years we have not been that kind of country.

Arthur Schlesinger Jr., *Los Angeles Times*, August 15, 2002.

In contemplating this geopolitical vision for the future, one wonders what happened to candidate Bush's rhetoric about the importance of "humility" in defining America's role in the world. Of course, he was then trying to downsize the humanitarian diplomacy attributed (mostly wrongly) to [democrats Bill Clinton and Al Gore], but the contrast in tone and substance is still striking. One wonders whether the heady atmosphere of the Oval Office has fed these geopolitical dreams, or whether our President, well-known for his lack of foreign policy knowledge, has been manipulated into a crusading mode by bureaucratic hawks who seized the opportunity so tragically provided by September 11.

An American Global Empire

Many influential Americans share this dream of a borderless global empire but adopt less forthright language. For instance, the respected military commentator Eliot Cohen, writing in a recent issue of *Foreign Affairs*, suggests that "in the twenty-first century, characterized like the European Middle Ages by a universal (if problematic) high culture with a universal language, the U.S. military plays an extraordinary and inimitable role. It has become, whether Americans or others like it or not, the ultimate guarantor of international order." To make such an assertion without apology or justification is to say, in effect, that the imperial role of the United States is no longer in doubt, or even subject to useful debate. To acknowledge that it makes no difference whether Americans or others support this destiny is to reveal the fallen condition of democracy and the irrelevance of international public opinion. Along similar lines of presupposition, Stephen Biddle, in the same issue of *Foreign Affairs*, observes in relation to the problems of the Balkans, and specifically Kosovo, that "Americans do well in crusades," but then he cites Cohen and Andrew Bacevich to the effect that "they are not suited . . . to the dirty work of imperial policing to secure second- or third-tier interest." Such an outlook makes the fact of an American global empire a foregone conclusion.

But pre-emption and double standards were not the only troubling features of this postmodern geopolitical outlook outlined in the West Point speech. There is first of all the issue of global dominance, a project to transform the world order from its current assemblage of sovereign states in the direction of a postmodern (that is, nonterritorial) global empire administered from Washington. Bush misleadingly assured the graduating cadets that "America has no empire to extend or utopia to establish," and then went on to describe precisely such undertakings. The President mentioned that past rivalries among states arose because of their efforts to compete with one another, but insisted that the future will be different because of American military superiority: "America has, and intends to keep, military strengths beyond challenge, thereby making the destabilizing arms races of other eras pointless, and limiting rivalries to trade and other pursuits of peace." The ambition here is breathtaking and imperial—nothing less than to remind all states that the era of self-help security is essentially over, that America is the global gendarme, and that other states should devote their energies to economic and peaceful pursuits, leaving overall security in Washington's hands. One can only wonder at the reaction of foreign ministries around the world, say in Paris or Beijing, when confronted by this language, which dramatically diminishes traditional sovereign rights, as well as by the reinforcing moves to scrap the Anti-Ballistic Missile treaty, to build a missile defense shield and to plan for the weaponization of space.

Whether it is Bush at West Point, or the more sedate writings of the foreign policy elite writing for each other, or for that matter intelligent and progressive criticism, useful analysis must proceed from the postmodern realization that we are addressing a menacing nonstate adversary concealed in a network that is simultaneously everywhere and nowhere. These new circumstances definitely call for new thinking that adapts international law and global security in an effective and constructive manner. But the adjustments called for by Bush do not meet the specific challenge of mega-terrorism, and they unleash a variety of dangerous forces. What is needed is new thinking that sees the United States as part of a global community that is seeking appropriate ways to restore security and confidence, but builds on existing frameworks of legal restraints and works toward a more robust UN, while not claiming for itself an imperial role to make up the rules of world politics as it goes along. Given the bipartisan gridlock that has gripped the country since September 11, positive forms of new thinking will almost certainly come, if they come, from pressures exerted by the citizenry outside the Beltway. We as citizens have never faced a more urgent duty.

"America needs a unified homeland security structure that will improve protection against today's threats and be flexible enough to help meet the unknown threats of the future."

The Department of Homeland Security Will Protect America Against Terrorists

George W. Bush

In the following viewpoint, originally given as a speech before the U.S. House of Representatives in June 2002, President George W. Bush outlines his plan for creating the Department of Homeland Security. Bush argues that the existing loose structure of government agencies created in the 1940s to respond to the Cold War is insufficient for addressing new terrorist threats. He claims that the new department—which will consolidate many agencies into one central department—will minimize duplication of efforts, improve coordination between agencies, and take advantage of advances in technology and management techniques. The bill creating the new department was signed into law in November 2002.

As you read, consider the following questions:
1. According to Bush, what would be the department's four main divisions?
2. How does Bush characterize America's terrorist enemies?

George W. Bush, "Message to Congress Transmitting Proposed Legislation to Create the Department of Homeland Security," *Weekly Compilation of Presidential Documents*, vol. 38, June 18, 2002.

I hereby transmit to the Congress proposed legislation to create a new Cabinet Department of Homeland Security.

Our Nation faces a new and changing threat unlike any we have faced before—the global threat of terrorism. No nation is immune, and all nations must act decisively to protect against this constantly evolving threat.

We must recognize that the threat of terrorism is a permanent condition, and we must take action to protect America against the terrorists that seek to kill the innocent.

Since September 11, 2001, all levels of government and leaders from across the political spectrum have cooperated like never before. We have strengthened our aviation security and tightened our borders. We have stockpiled medicines to defend against bio-terrorism and improved our ability to combat weapons of mass destruction. We have dramatically improved information sharing among our intelligence agencies, and we have taken new steps to protect our critical infrastructure.

We Can Do Better

Our Nation is stronger and better prepared today than it was on September 11. Yet, we can do better. I propose the most extensive reorganization of the Federal Government since the 1940s by creating a new Department of Homeland Security. For the first time we would have a single Department whose primary mission is to secure our homeland. Soon after the Second World War, President Harry Truman recognized that our Nation's fragmented military defenses needed reorganization to help win the Cold War. President Truman proposed uniting our military forces under a single entity, now the Department of Defense, and creating the National Security Council to bring together defense, intelligence, and diplomacy. President Truman's reforms are still helping us to fight terror abroad, and today we need similar dramatic reforms to secure our people at home.

President Truman and Congress reorganized our Government to meet a very visible enemy in the Cold War. Today our Nation must once again reorganize our Government to protect against an often-invisible enemy, an enemy that hides in the shadows and an enemy that can strike with many different types of weapons. Our enemies seek to obtain the most dangerous and deadly weapons of mass destruction and use them against the innocent. While we are winning the war on terrorism, Al Qaeda and other terrorist organizations still have thousands of trained killers spread across the globe plotting attacks against America and the other nations of the civilized world.

Immediately after last fall's attack, I used my legal authority to establish the White House Office of Homeland Security and the Homeland Security Council to help ensure that our Federal response and protection efforts were coordinated and effective. I also directed Homeland Security Advisor Tom Ridge to study the Federal Government as a whole to determine if the current structure allows us to meet the threats of today while preparing for the unknown threats of tomorrow. After careful study of the current structure, coupled with the experience gained since September 11 and new information we have learned about our enemies while fighting a war, I have concluded that our Nation needs a more unified homeland security structure.

I propose to create a new Department of Homeland Security by substantially transforming the current confusing patchwork of government activities into a single department whose primary mission is to secure our homeland. My proposal builds on the strong bipartisan work on the issue of homeland security that has been conducted by Members of Congress. In designing the new Department, my Administration considered a number of homeland security organizational proposals that have emerged from outside studies, commissions, and Members of Congress.

The Need for a Department of Homeland Security

Today no Federal Government agency has homeland security as its primary mission. Responsibilities for homeland security are dispersed among more than 100 different entities of the Federal Government. America needs a unified homeland security structure that will improve protection against today's threats and be flexible enough to help meet the unknown threats of the future.

Organization of the Department of Homeland Security

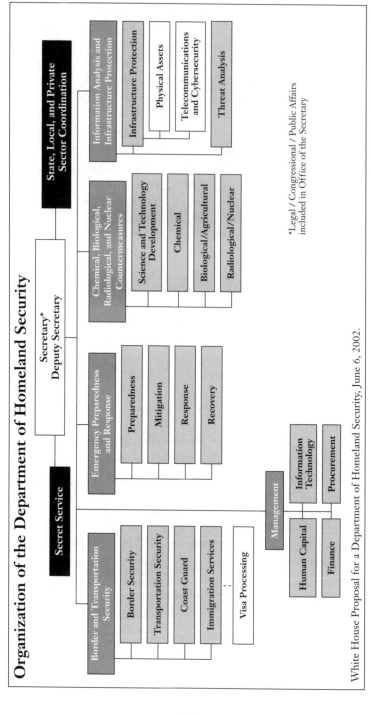

White House Proposal for a Department of Homeland Security, June 6, 2002.

138

The mission of the new Department would be to prevent terrorist attacks within the United States, to reduce America's vulnerability to terrorism, and to minimize the damage and recover from attacks that may occur. The Department of Homeland Security would mobilize and focus the resources of the Federal Government, State and local governments, the private sector, and the American people to accomplish its mission.

One Department

The Department of Homeland Security would make Americans safer because for the first time we would have one department dedicated to securing the homeland. One department would secure our borders, transportation sector, ports, and critical infrastructure. One department would analyze homeland security intelligence from multiple sources, synthesize it with a comprehensive assessment of America's vulnerabilities, and take action to secure our highest risk facilities and systems. One department would coordinate communications with State and local governments, private industry, and the American people about threats and preparedness. One department would coordinate our efforts to secure the American people against bioterrorism and other weapons of mass destruction. One department would help train and equip our first responders. One department would manage Federal emergency response activities.

Our goal is not to expand Government, but to create an agile organization that takes advantage of modern technology and management techniques to meet a new and constantly evolving threat. We can improve our homeland security by minimizing the duplication of efforts, improving coordination, and combining functions that are currently fragmented and inefficient. The new Department would allow us to have more security officers in the field working to stop terrorists and fewer resources in Washington managing duplicative activities that drain critical homeland security resources.

The Department of Homeland Security would have a clear and efficient organizational structure with four main divisions: Border and Transportation Security; Emergency Preparedness and Response; Chemical, Biological, Radiological and Nuclear Countermeasures; and Information Analysis and Infrastructure Protection. . . .

The Lessons of History

History teaches us that new challenges require new organizational structures. History also teaches us that critical security challenges require clear lines of responsibility and the unified effort of the U.S. Government.

President Truman said, looking at the lessons of the Second World War: "It is now time to discard obsolete organizational forms, and to provide for the future the soundest, the most effective, and the most economical kind of structure for our armed forces." When skeptics told President Truman that this proposed reorganization was too ambitious to be enacted, he simply replied that it had to be. In the years to follow, the Congress acted upon President Truman's recommendation, eventually laying a sound organizational foundation that enabled the United States to win the Cold War. All Americans today enjoy the inheritance of this landmark organizational reform: a unified Department of Defense that has become the most powerful force for freedom the world has ever seen.

Today America faces a threat that is wholly different from the threat we faced during the Cold War. Our terrorist enemies hide in shadows and attack civilians with whatever means of destruction they can access. But as in the Cold War, meeting this threat requires clear lines of responsibility and the unified efforts of government at all levels—Federal, State, local, and tribal—the private sector, and all Americans. America needs a homeland security establishment that can help prevent catastrophic attacks and mobilize national resources for an enduring conflict while protecting our Nation's values and liberties.

Years from today, our world will still be fighting the threat of terrorism. It is my hope that future generations will be able to look back on the Homeland Security Act of 2002—as we now remember the National Security Act of 1947—as the solid organizational foundation for America's triumph in a long and difficult struggle against a formidable enemy.

History has given our Nation new challenges—and important new assignments. Only the United States Congress can create a new department of Government. We face an urgent need, and I am pleased that Congress has responded to my call to act before the end of the current congressional session with the same bipartisan spirit that allowed us to act expeditiously on legislation after September 11.

These are times that demand bipartisan action and bipartisan solutions to meet the new and changing threats we face as a Nation. I urge the Congress to join me in creating a single, permanent department with an overriding and urgent mission—securing the homeland of America and protecting the American people. Together we can meet this ambitious deadline and help ensure that the American homeland is secure against the terrorist threat.

> "Congress is actually jeopardizing the security of millions of Americans . . . to rearrange deck chairs and give big spenders yet another department on which to lavish pork-barrel spending."

The Department of Homeland Security Will Make America Less Safe

Ron Paul

In the following address, originally given before the House of Representatives in July 2002, Texas representative Ron Paul argues against a bill authorizing the creation of the Department of Homeland Security. He claims that the new department—which consolidates many government agencies into one centralized department—will actually make Americans less safe by diverting critical resources from fighting terrorism to rearranging government offices and command structures. Moreover, Paul contends that creating the new department will result in more government controls over the lives of individual Americans. The bill was eventually passed by Congress and signed by the president in November 2002.

As you read, consider the following questions:

1. How many government agencies will comprise the new Department of Homeland Security, as reported by Paul?
2. According to the author, how much money is needed to implement the new department?

Ron Paul, address before the U.S. House of Representatives, July 26, 2002.

As many commentators have pointed out, the creation of [the Department of Homeland Security] represents the largest reorganization of Federal agencies since the creation of the Department of Defense in 1947. Unfortunately, the process by which we are creating this new department bears little resemblance to the process by which the Defense Department was created.[1]

The Problems with New Departments

Congress began hearings on the proposed department of defense in 1945—two years before President Harry S. Truman signed legislation creating the new department into law. Despite the lengthy deliberative process through which Congress created the new department, turf battles and logistical problems continued to bedevil the military establishment, requiring several corrective pieces of legislation. In fact, the Goldwater-Nichols Department of Defense Reorganization Act of 1986 (PL 99-433) was passed to deal with problems stemming from the 1947 law. The experience with the Department of Defense certainly suggests the importance of a more deliberative process in the creation of this new agency.

This current proposed legislation suggests that merging 22 government agencies and departments—comprising nearly 200,000 Federal employees—into one department will address our current vulnerabilities. I do not see how this can be the case.

If we are presently under terrorist threat, it seems to me that turning 22 agencies upside down, sparking scores of turf wars, and creating massive logistical and technological headaches—does anyone really believe that even simple things like computer and telephone networks will be up and running in the short term?—is hardly the way to maintain the readiness and focus necessary to defend the United States.

What about vulnerabilities while Americans wait for this massive new bureaucracy to begin functioning as a whole even to the levels at which its component parts were functioning before this legislation was taken up? Is this a risk we

---

1. The Senate voted in favor of creating the Department of Homeland Security in November 2002.

can afford to take? Also, isn't it a bit ironic that in the name of "homeland security" we seem to be consolidating everything except the government agencies most critical to the defense of the United States, the multitude of intelligence agencies that make up the intelligence community?

Local Concerns

I come from a coastal district in Texas. The Coast Guard and its mission are important to us. The chairman of the committee of jurisdiction over the Coast Guard has expressed strong reservations about the plan to move the Coast Guard into the new department. Recently my district was hit by the flooding in Texas, and we relied upon the Federal Emergency Management Agency to again provide certain services. Additionally, as a district close to our border, much of the casework performed in my district offices relates to requests made to the Immigration and Naturalization Service (INS).

There has been a difference of opinion between committees of jurisdiction and the administration in regard to all these functions. In fact, the President's proposal was amended in no fewer than a half dozen of the dozen committees to which it was originally referred.

My coastal district also relies heavily on shipping. Our ports are essential for international trade and commerce. In 2001, over one million tons of goods was moved through just one of the ports in my district. However, questions remain about how the mission of the Customs Service will be changed by this new department.

For me to vote for this bill would amount to giving my personal assurance that the creation of this new department will not adversely impact the fashion in which the Coast Guard and Customs Service provide the services which my constituents have come to rely upon. Based on the expedited process we have followed with this legislation, I do not believe I can give such assurance.

Misspent Resources

We have also received a Congressional Budget Office cost estimate suggesting that it will cost no less than $3 billion just to implement this new department. That is $3 billion that could be spent to capture those responsible for the [September 11, 2001, terrorist attacks on America] or to provide tax relief to the families of the victims of that attack. It is $3 billion that could perhaps be better spent protecting against future attacks, or simply to meet the fiscal needs of our government.

Since those attacks this Congress has gone on a massive spending spree. Spending three billion additional dollars now, simply to rearrange offices and command structures, is not a wise move. In fact, Congress is actually jeopardizing the security of millions of Americans by raiding the Social Security trust fund to rearrange deck chairs and give big spenders yet another department on which to lavish pork-barrel spending.

Stein. © 2002 by Rocky Mountain News. Reprinted by permission.

The way the costs of this department have skyrocketed before the department is even open for business leads me to fear that this will become yet another justification for Congress to raid the Social Security trust fund in order to finance pork-barrel spending. This is especially true in light of the fact that so many questions remain regarding the ultimate effect of these structural changes.

Moreover, this legislation will give the Executive Branch the authority to spend money appropriated by Congress in ways Congress has not authorized. This clearly erodes constitutionally mandated congressional prerogatives relative to control of Federal spending.

More Government Control

The airlines are bailed out and given guaranteed insurance against all threats. We have made the airline industry a public utility that gets to keep its profits and pass on its losses to the taxpayers, like Amtrak and the post office. Instead of more ownership responsibility, we get more government controls. I am reluctant, to say the least, to give any new powers to bureaucrats who refuse to recognize the vital role free citizens exercising their Second Amendment rights play in homeland security.

Government reorganizations, though generally seen as benign, can have a deleterious effect not just on the functioning of government but on our safety and liberty as well. The concentration and centralization of authority that may result from today's efforts should give us all reason for pause. But the current process does not allow for pause. Indeed, it militates toward rushing decisions without regard to consequence.

Furthermore, this particular reorganization, in an attempt to provide broad leeway for the new department, undermines our congressional oversight function. Abrogating our constitutionally mandated responsibilities so hastily now also means that future administrations will find it much easier to abuse the powers of this new department to violate constitutional liberties.

Perhaps a streamlined, reconfigured Federal Government with a more clearly defined and limited mission focused on protecting citizens and their freedoms could result from this reorganization, but right now it seems far more likely that the opposite will occur. That is why I must oppose creation of this new department.

Until we deal with the substance of the problem—serious issues of American foreign policy about which I have spoken out for years, and important concerns with our immigration policy in light of the current environment—attempts such as we undertake today at improved homeland security will amount to, more or less, rearranging deck chairs—or perhaps more accurately office chairs in various bureaucracies.

Until we are prepared to have serious and frank discussions of policy, this body will not improve the security of American citizens and their property. I stand ready to have that debate, but unfortunately this bill does nothing to begin the debate and nothing substantive to protect us. At best it will provide an illusion of security, and at worst these unanswered questions will be resolved by the realization that entities such as the Customs Service, Coast Guard, and INS will be less effective, less efficient, more intrusive, and mired in more bureaucratic red tape.

> "*Alternative societies' that mass immigration has created [allow] alien terrorists to live and operate without being noticed.*"

Immigration Must Be Restricted to Protect America Against Terrorists

Samuel Francis

In the following viewpoint syndicated columnist Samuel Francis contends that mass immigration to the United States makes it easier for terrorists—such as those responsible for the September 11, 2001, terrorist attacks—to operate. According to Francis, many urban communities have been overrun with foreign-born residents, creating ideal "staging areas" for Middle Eastern terrorists to hide and plan their attacks. Francis claims that the best way to reduce the terrorist threat is to close the nation's borders.

As you read, consider the following questions:

1. In Francis's opinion, what are the two dimensions of the relationship between immigration and the September 11, 2001, terrorist attacks?
2. How many identifiable nationalities exist in Patterson, New Jersey, as reported by the author?
3. According to British researcher R. Gunaratna, why do Muslim fundamentalist groups thrive in the Netherlands?

Samuel Francis, "The Enemy Is Here—Not Afghanistan," *Conservative Chronicle*, vol. 16, October 10, 2001, p. 7. Copyright © 2001 by Creators Syndicate. Reproduced by permission.

By an overwhelming majority of 77 percent, the American public believes "the government is not doing enough to control the border and screen people allowed into the country," according to a Zogby poll just released [in October 2001]. The American public, in other words, has learned something from the Sept. 11 [2001] terrorist attack, if indeed it ever believed otherwise. But there has yet to be any suggestion from the American leadership class, political or cultural, that it has learned anything at all.

Two Dimensions to the Problem

There are two dimensions to the relationship between immigration and the attacks. One is the problem of loopholes and lax security measures in our current laws and entry procedures. That sort of thing is receiving attention and is, relatively speaking, easy enough to fix with more money, training and personnel, and tighter regulations. Fixing it doesn't seriously reverse the mass immigration-open borders policies that have prevailed over the last 30 years:

The other dimension does affect those policies and is far more difficult to fix, for at least two reasons to be mentioned anon. This dimension concerns what I have termed the "alternative societies" that mass immigration has created and which allow alien terrorists to live and operate without being noticed. The *New York Times* . . . carried a story about just such a society in New Jersey, where four of the 19 Sept. 11 mass killers hung out.

"In this neighborhood of Latinos, African-Americans and recent immigrants speaking dozens of languages," the *Times* reported of Patterson, New Jersey, "the handful of young Arab men who came and went drew almost no notice. In their apartment above a bodega, they did not play loud music. They appeared not to speak English."

The area was "one of several East Coast staging areas for the attacks on the World Trade Center and the Pentagon," and the "hijackers' stay here also shows how, in an area that speaks many languages and keeps absorbing immigrants, a few young men with no apparent means of support and no furniture can settle in for months without drawing attention."

Patterson's mayor notes: "We have 72 identifiable nationalities here, 170,000 people in eight square miles. With a lot of different folks moving in and out of the city, unless you raise a ruckus, you could live here for a while without anyone noticing."

Lessons from Other Nations

Nor is the United States alone in its enjoyment of such diversity; Europe, too, has its immigrant subcultures. Holland, for example, is a country where Osama bin Laden's cadres have been able to take advantage of the "cultural tolerance" that mass immigration both demands and supplies.

British researcher Dr. R. Gunaratna warns that, "especially in the Netherlands, because of its total lack of anti-terrorism laws and its very high level of religious, cultural and judicial tolerance, Muslim-fundamentalist terrorist groups are allowed to thrive. They use Amsterdam and Rotterdam as central bases in the West from which they garnish funds, recruit activists from the local Muslim youth cultural groups and purchase highly sophisticated arms in the world's largest trading hub: Rotterdam harbor." There are several lessons, fairly obvious to most Americans, to be drawn from such facts.

Public Opinion on Immigration Services

Do you think the government is doing enough to control the border and to screen people allowed into the country?

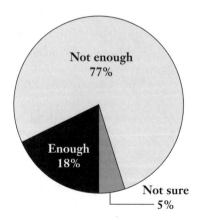

Center for Immigration Studies, September 2001.

Lesson One is that the enemy is not in Afghanistan; the enemy is here. Precisely because of mass immigration and open-borders policies, perhaps thousands of unnoticeable young men have been able to enter the United States (and Europe) to prepare jihad against their enemies. Short of expelling entire populations in a massive act of ethnic cleansing, there is virtually nothing the United States and the West can do about the new enemy within.

That brings us to Lesson Two, and back to why this dimension of the immigration problem is so hard to repair. The leadership class of the United States and the West simply is not prepared to embark on such a campaign of ethnic cleansing; even many "closed borders" advocates shrink from supporting such a policy, simply because of the suffering and uprooting that would be involved.

But Lesson Three is that at least we can start by closing the borders now and doing what we can to root out the terrorists and their comrades. Unfortunately, the leadership class won't allow that, either.

It won't allow it because closing the borders and halting immigration would thwart its own interests and ideology— its need for cheap labor, a new underclass, and a multiculturalist and globalist hegemonic doctrine. The reason we have mass immigration is that the ruling class wants it, regardless of what the American public wants, and that's also the reason why in all the palaver about how to control terrorism and all the restrictions on liberty, wiretapping, surveillance, possible assassinations and outright wars we have to endure, establish, permit and wage, hardly once has any member of the ruling class suggested that we halt or even reduce immigration.

"*Drastically reducing the number of foreigners who enter the United States . . . would compound the economic damage of [the September 11, 2001, terrorist attacks] while doing nothing to enhance our security.*"

Restricting Immigration Will Not Make America Safer

Daniel T. Griswold

Daniel T. Griswold argues in the following viewpoint that restricting immigration to the United States would harm the nation, not make it safer. According to Griswold, terrorists such as those responsible for the September 11, 2001, terrorist attacks do not enter the country as immigrants but as aliens on temporary tourist and student visas, so restricting immigration would have no effect on their movements. However, restricting immigration would harm the economy by reducing the number of foreign-born workers who enable U.S. producers to keep prices down and prosper in the global economy. Daniel T. Griswold is the associate director of the Cato Institute's Center for Trade Policy Studies and the author of many articles on trade and immigration.

As you read, consider the following questions:
1. How does Griswold counter the claim that immigration to the United States causes overpopulation problems?
2. What percentage of foreign nationals entering the United States come to immigrate, according to the author?
3. How does the author characterize the difference between America's Mexican and Canadian borders?

I mmigration always has been controversial in the United States. More than two centuries ago, Benjamin Franklin worried that too many German immigrants would swamp America's predominantly British culture. In the mid-1800s, Irish immigrants were scorned as lazy drunks, not to mention Roman Catholics. At the turn of the century a wave of "new immigrants"—Poles, Italians, Russian Jews—were believed to be too different ever to assimilate into American life. Today the same fears are raised about immigrants from Latin America and Asia, but current critics of immigration are as wrong as their counterparts were in previous eras.

Immigration is not undermining the American experiment; it is an integral part of it. We are a nation of immigrants. Successive waves of immigrants have kept our country demographically young, enriched our culture and added to our productive capacity as a nation, enhancing our influence in the world.

Immigration gives the United States an economic edge in the world economy. Immigrants bring innovative ideas and entrepreneurial spirit to the U.S. economy. They provide business contacts to other markets, enhancing America's ability to trade and invest profitably in the global economy. They keep our economy flexible, allowing U.S. producers to keep prices down and to respond to changing consumer demands. An authoritative 1997 study by the National Academy of Sciences (NAS) concluded that immigration delivered a "significant positive gain" to the U.S. economy. In testimony before Congress, Federal Reserve Board Chairman Alan Greenspan said, "I've always argued that this country has benefited immensely from the fact that we draw people from all over the world."

Contrary to popular myth, immigrants do not push Americans out of jobs. Immigrants tend to fill jobs that Americans cannot or will not fill, mostly at the high and low ends of the skill spectrum. Immigrants are disproportionately represented in such high-skilled fields as medicine, physics and computer science, but also in lower-skilled sectors such as hotels and restaurants, domestic service, construction and light manufacturing.

Immigrants also raise demand for goods as well as the supply. During the long boom of the 1990s, and especially in the second half of the decade, the national unemployment rate fell below 4 percent and real wages rose up and down the income scale during a time of relatively high immigration.

Nowhere is the contribution of immigrants more apparent than in the high-technology and other knowledge-based sectors. Silicon Valley and other high-tech sectors would cease to function if we foolishly were to close our borders to skilled and educated immigrants. These immigrants represent human capital that can make our entire economy more productive. Immigrants have developed new products, such as the Java computer language, that have created employment opportunities for millions of Americans.

Many Claims Refuted

Immigrants are not a drain on government finances. The NAS study found that the typical immigrant and his or her offspring will pay a net $80,000 more in taxes during their lifetimes than they collect in government services. For immigrants with college degrees, the net fiscal return is $198,000. It is true that low-skilled immigrants and refugees tend to use welfare more than the typical "native" household, but the 1996 Welfare Reform Act made it much more difficult for newcomers to collect welfare. As a result, immigrant use of welfare has declined in recent years along with overall welfare rolls.

Despite the claims of immigration opponents, today's flow is not out of proportion to historical levels. Immigration in the last decade has averaged about 1 million per year, high in absolute numbers, but the rate of 4 immigrants per year per 1,000 U.S. residents is less than half the rate during the Great Migration of 1890–1914. Today, about 10 percent of U.S. residents are foreign-born, an increase from 4.7 percent in 1970, but still far short of the 14.7 percent who were foreign-born in 1910.

Nor can immigrants fairly be blamed for causing "over-population." America's annual population growth of 1 percent is below our average growth rate of the last century. In fact, without immigration our labor force would begin to shrink within two decades. According to the 2000 Census, 22 percent of U.S. counties lost population between 1990 and 2000. Immigrants could help revitalize demographically declining areas of the country, just as they helped revitalize New York City and other previously declining urban centers.

An Inappropriate Response to Terrorist Attacks

Drastically reducing the number of foreigners who enter the United States each year only would compound the economic damage of [the September 11, 2001, terrorist attacks on America] while doing nothing to enhance our security. The tourist industry, already reeling, would lose millions of foreign visitors, and American universities would lose hundreds of thousands of foreign students if our borders were closed.

Obviously the U.S. government should "control its borders" to keep out anyone who intends to commit terrorist acts. The problem is not that we are letting too many people into the United States but that the government has failed to keep the wrong people out. We can stop terrorists from entering the United States without closing our borders or reducing the number of hardworking, peaceful immigrants who settle here.

America Does Not Need a Berlin Wall

The only permanent solution to terrorism against the United States is to address the flaws in U.S. foreign policy, which is the breeding ground for terrorism against our country. No immigration controls in the world, not even a rebuilt Berlin Wall around the United States, will succeed in preventing the entry of people who are bound and determined to kill Americans.

Jacob G. Hornberger, *World & I*, January 2002.

We must do whatever is necessary to stop potentially dangerous people at the border. Law-enforcement and intelligence agencies must work closely with the State Department, the Immigration and Naturalization Service (INS) and U.S. Customs to share real-time information about potential terrorists. Computer systems must be upgraded and new technologies adopted to screen out the bad guys without causing intolerable delays at the border. More agents need to be posted at ports of entry to more thoroughly screen for high-risk travelers. We must bolster cooperation with our neighbors, Canada and Mexico, to ensure that terrorists cannot slip across our long land borders.

In the wake of September 11, longtime critics of immigration have tried to exploit legitimate concerns about security to argue for drastic cuts in immigration. But border security and immigration are two separate matters. Immigrants are only a small subset of the total number of foreigners who enter the United States every year. Only about one of every 25 foreign nationals who enter the United States come here to immigrate. The rest are tourists, business travelers, students and Mexicans and Canadians who cross the border for a weekend to shop or visit family and then return home with no intention of settling permanently in the United States.

The 19 terrorists who attacked the United States on Sept. 11 did not apply to the INS to immigrate or to become U.S. citizens. Like most aliens who enter the United States, they were here on temporary tourist and student visas. We could reduce the number of immigrants to zero and still not stop terrorists from slipping into the country on nonimmigrant visas.

To defend ourselves better against terrorism, our border-control system requires a reorientation of mission. For the last two decades, U.S. immigration policy has been obsessed with nabbing mostly Mexican-born workers whose only "crime" is their desire to earn an honest day's pay. Those workers pose no threat to national security.

Border Problems

Our land border with Mexico is half as long as our border with Canada, yet before September 11 it was patrolled by 10 times as many border agents. On average we were posting an agent every five miles along our 3,987-mile border with Canada and every quarter-mile on the 2,000-mile border with Mexico. On the Northern border there were 120,000 entries per year per agent compared with 40,000 entries on the Southwestern border. This is out of proportion to any legitimate fears about national security. In fact terrorists seem to prefer the northern border. Let's remember that it was at a border-crossing station in Washington state in December 1999 that a terrorist was apprehended with explosives that were to be used to blow up Los Angeles International Airport during the millennium celebrations.

At a February 2000 hearing, former Senator Slade Gorton (R-Wash.) warned that "understaffing at our northern border is jeopardizing the security of our nation, not to mention border personnel, while in at least some sections of the southern border, there are so many agents that there is not enough work to keep them all busy."

We should stop wasting scarce resources in a self-destructive quest to hunt down Mexican construction workers and raid restaurants and chicken-processing plants, and redirect those resources to track potential terrorists and smash their cells before they can blow up more buildings and kill more Americans.

For all these reasons, President George W. Bush's initiative to legalize and regularize the movement of workers across the U.S.-Mexican border makes sense in terms of national security as well as economics. It also is politically smart.

In his latest book, *The Death of the West*, Pat Buchanan argues that opposing immigration will be a winning formula for conservative Republicans. His own political decline and fall undermine his claim. Like former liberal Republican Governor Pete Wilson in California, Buchanan has tried to win votes by blaming immigration for America's problems. But voters wisely rejected Buchanan's thesis. Despite $12 million in taxpayer campaign funds, and an assist from the Florida butterfly ballot, Buchanan won less than 0.5 percent of the presidential vote in 2000. In contrast Bush, by affirming immigration, raised the GOP's share of the Hispanic vote to 35 percent from the 21 percent carried by Bob Dole in 1996. If conservatives adopt the anti-immigrant message, they risk following Buchanan and Wilson into political irrelevancy.

It would be a national shame if, in the name of security, we closed the door to immigrants who come here to work, save and build a better life for themselves and their families. Immigrants come here to live the American Dream; terrorists come to destroy it. We should not allow America's tradition of welcoming immigrants to become yet another casualty of September 11.

Periodical Bibliography

The following articles have been selected to supplement the diverse views presented in this chapter.

George W. Bush	"Commencement Address at the U.S. Military Academy in West Point, New York," *Weekly Compilation of Presidential Documents*, June 10, 2002.
Steven Camarota	"Borders and Terrorism," *Social Contract*, Winter 2002.
Linda Chavez	"Don't Seal the Borders," *Wall Street Journal*, November 21, 2001.
Michael Duffy	"Does Might Make Right? With His Aggressive Military Doctrine, Bush Is Asking for Too Much Trust, *Time*, September 30, 2002.
Jacob G. Hornberger	"Keep the Borders Open," *World & I*, January 2002.
Lamar Jacoby	"Don't Slam the Door," *Reader's Digest*, March 2002.
Mary Kaldor	"Winning a New Kind of War," *Utne Reader*, January/February 2002.
Marl Krikorian	"U.S. Immigration? Still a Bad Idea," *World & I*, January 2002.
Sarah McCarthy	"Time to Fight," *Liberty*, November 2001.
Kate O'Breirne	"The DHS Debate: A Department We'll Spend a Lifetime Criticizing," *National Review*, August 12, 2002.
Arthur Schlesinger Jr.	"The Immorality of Preventative War," *Los Angeles Times*, August 15, 2002.
Philip Shenon	"Establishing New Agency Is Expected to Take Years and Could Divert It from Mission," *New York Times*, November 20, 2002.
Scott Simon	"Reflections of the Events of September Eleventh," *Friends Journal*, December 2001.
Spectator	"America Must Fight Back," September 15, 2001.
J. Michael Waller	"A Wartime Window of Opportunity," *Insight on the News*, February 4, 2002.
Howard Zinn	"Compassion, Not Vengeance," *Progressive Populist*, October 15, 2001.

CHAPTER 4

Do Efforts to Enhance National Security Threaten Civil Liberties?

Chapter Preface

In George Orwell's dystopian novel *1984*, the authoritarian federal government controls every aspect of people's lives. This government is represented by Big Brother, who monitors each person's movements and thoughts using sophisticated surveillance technology. Ostensibly these measures are necessary to protect the nation from its enemies, the threat of which is regularly exaggerated in the government-controlled media.

Since America's enemies crashed commercial airliners into the World Trade Center and the Pentagon on September 11, 2001, the U.S. government has undertaken efforts to enhance national security, many of which have prompted charges that Big Brother is alive and well. Many commentators maintain that following the attacks, U.S. government officials began exaggerating future threats to America's security in order to justify giving government more power over citizens. These analysts argue that current efforts to guard America against future terrorist acts threaten a number of specific liberties its citizens take for granted, such as freedom of movement, freedom from harassment, and anonymity. The list of contested measures is long: airport full-body searches, detainment of immigrants suspected of knowing terrorists, monitoring of individuals' e-mail and other Internet activity, and approved wiretaps, among others. As Orwell's novel makes clear, governments that exercise complete control over their citizenry can implement whatever policies are deemed necessary to protect the nation from outside threats. However, in a free society, citizens can voice their concerns about such policies if they appear to threaten basic liberties.

Most Americans doubtless feel that their country is the antithesis of the society Orwell describes in his novel. Indeed, early in the American experiment Thomas Jefferson articulated the values that would define America: "We hold these truths to be self-evident, that all men are created equal, that they are endowed by their Creator with certain inalienable Rights, that among these are Life, Liberty, and the pursuit of Happiness." Living in "the land of the free," Americans are particularly sensitive about protecting civil liberties. For many, exchanging basic freedoms for greater security threatens the essence of what America stands for. They assert that an erosion of civil liberties poses more of a risk to the nation than any external threat. Senator Russ Feingold puts it this way: "Of course there is no doubt that, if we lived in a police state, it would be easier to catch terrorists. . . . But that probably would not be a country in which we would want to live. . . . That would not be America."

However, others point out that modern threats to America's security demand greater protections, which necessitate some curtailment of civil liberties. Such a tradeoff, they believe, is in the best interests of the nation. These commentators point out that the nature of threats to America's security have changed since the Cold War, and the nation's security methods must change as well. New threats come from mobile terrorist cells operating anonymously over the Internet, not from established nation-states. Some experts contend that efforts to protect civil liberties are undermining the nation's ability to protect itself. Attorney General John Ashcroft exclaims, "To those who scare peace-loving people with phantoms of lost liberty, my message is this: Your tactics only aid terrorists—for they erode our national unity."

In the aftermath of the September 11 attacks, policy makers must constantly weigh the cost of heightened protection against the attendant loss of freedom. The authors in the following chapter discuss whether or not efforts to enhance national security pose a risk to civil liberties. To be sure, the specter of an all-powerful government frightens many Americans more than terrorism itself. Over fifty years ago, Orwell captured their fears with the slogan "BIG BROTHER IS WATCHING YOU."

> *"How wrong . . . that we've dealt away some of our freedom and privacy for a promise of safety and security."*

Efforts to Enhance National Security Threaten Civil Liberties

Nick Gillespie

According to Nick Gillespie in the following viewpoint, trading freedom and privacy for enhanced security is a bad swap. In doing so, he contends, Americans are dishonoring those who died in the September 11, 2001, terrorist attacks and sacrificing the values for which America stands. Gillespie argues, for example, that the anti-terrorism legislation passed immediately after the attacks allows law enforcement to spy on U.S. citizens. When people sacrifice freedom for security in times of crisis, he maintains, they unwittingly pave the way for ever more restrictions on their civil liberties. Nick Gillespie is editor in chief of *Reason*, a libertarian magazine.

As you read, consider the following questions:

1. What percentage of respondents in a Gallup/University of Oklahoma poll favored trading civil liberties for security, as cited by Gillespie?
2. As reported by the author, what law enforcement activities does the USA PATRIOT Act sanction?
3. What violations of civil liberties have Americans become accustomed to since the September 11, 2001, terrorist attacks, in the author's opinion?

Nick Gillespie, "Freedom for Safety: An Old Trade—and a Useless One," *Reason*, vol. 34, October 2002, pp. 25–26. Copyright © 2002 by the Reason Foundation. Reproduced with permission.

A mid the mad, horrific carnage of [the September 11, 2001, terrorist attacks on America]—amid the planes screaming into office buildings and cornfields; amid the last-minute phone calls by doomed innocents to loved ones; amid the victims so desperate that they dove from the heights of the World Trade Center to the pavement below (what nightmare thoughts must have shot through their minds in that all too brief yet interminable fall to Ground Zero?); amid the billowing cloud of ash that smothered Manhattan and the rest of the country like a volcanic eruption of unmitigated human suffering; amid the heroism of plane passengers and firemen and cops and neighbors; amid the crush of steel and concrete and glass that flattened 220 stories into a pile barely 50 feet tall—amid the 3,000 deaths that day, something else died too.

A Bad Swap

By nightfall, it seemed, we had changed from a nation that placed a uniquely high value on privacy and freedom to one that embraced security and safety as first principles. Of *course* we swapped freedom for safety. Just look again at those people jumping from the twin towers to understand why 78 percent of respondents in a recent Gallup/University of Oklahoma poll favored trading civil liberties for "security" (and why 71 percent supported a national ID card too). Never mind that the trade hasn't made us safer, or that it erodes the freedom that we say is precisely what the terrorists hate about us.

Within days of the attacks, Attorney General John Ashcroft pushed Congress to pass expansive anti-terrorism legislation that was a lawman's wish list (and not very different from the regular requests made by lawmen before 9/11).We *must*, implored the man who had redirected FBI efforts away from counterterrorism and back toward battling drugs and kiddie porn, make it easier for cops and feds and spies to get the drop on suspects, broaden the definition of and increase the penalties for money laundering, impose new restrictions on immigration, and on and on.

On October 26, 2001, President George W. Bush signed the USA PATRIOT Act, an acronym for a law so ludicrously named that it sounds like [satirist] Thomas Pynchon parodying [dystopia author] George Orwell: the Uniting and Strengthening America by Providing Appropriate Tools Required to Intercept and Obstruct Terrorism Act. As the Electronic Frontier Foundation (EFF) and other critics noted, the legislation ran to 342 pages and made major changes to over a dozen statutes that had limited government surveillance of citizens. We can assume that many legislators and their staffers, in the time-honored tradition, didn't read the text before casting their votes. Likewise, it will be years, not just months, before the act's full implications are clear.

Markstein. © 2001 by Milwaukee Journal Sentinel. Reproduced by permission of Copley News Service.

The USA PATRIOT Act is a synecdoche for the freedom-for-safety swap. Among many other things, it sanctioned roving wiretaps (which allow police to track individuals over different phones and computers) and spying on the Web browsers of people who are not even criminal suspects. It rewrote the definitions of terrorism and money laundering to include all sorts of lesser and wider-ranging offenses. More important, as EFF underscored, "In asking for these broad new powers, the government made no showing that the previous powers of law enforcement and intelligence agencies to spy on U.S. citizens were insufficient to allow them to investigate and prosecute acts of terrorism." Nothing that's emerged in the past year contradicts that early assessment.

Never a Done Deal

"We're likely to experience more restrictions on personal freedom than has ever been the case in this country," pronounced Supreme Court Justice Sandra Day O'Connor last year after visiting Ground Zero. So we have, in ways large and small, profound and trivial. The worst part of the freedom-for-safety swap is that it's *never* a done deal; the safety providers are endless hagglers, always coming back for more. This fall's [2002] major homeland security legislation, unfinished at press time, will doubtless renew the negotiations.

Who knows where it will end? Freedom and privacy rarely, if ever, disappear in one fell swoop. In just a year, we've become accustomed to unnamed "detainees" being held in secret by the Department of Justice (and to the DOJ refusing to comply with state and federal court rulings to release the names of suspects); to the possibility of equally secret "military tribunals" (it's all right—they won't be used against U.S. citizens, except *maybe* "bad apples" like dirty bomb suspect Jose Padilla, and wasn't he a gang member anyway?); to state and federal agencies' dragging their feet on releasing documents legally available through open government laws; and to legislators such as Senator Mike DeWine (R-Ohio) constantly pushing the limits of the USA PATRIOT Act. (DeWine wants to allow the FBI to wiretap legal immigrants on the weakest "suspicion" of criminal activity.)

Trained to Relinquish Civil Rights

We've become trained to show up hours earlier to airports and to shuffle passively through security checkpoints, to unbuckle our pants and untuck our shirts, to hold our feet up in the air while agents wave wands over our shoes, to surrender nail clippers at the gate or just travel without them, to grin and bear it while Grandma's walker gets the once-over. (Who even remembers the relative ease of air travel pre-9/11— much less before the mid-'90s, when we first started showing picture IDs as a condition of flying?) We've already started to ignore the ubiquitous surveillance cameras like the ones that watched over us as we celebrated the Fourth of July on the Mall in Washington, D.C. We've learned to mock a never-ending series of proposals such as the infamous Operation Terrorist Information and Prevention System (TIPS) and plans for beefing up the old Neighborhood Watch program into a full-blown "national system for . . . reporting suspicious activity," both of which are moving forward in modified form despite widespread hooting.

Has any of this made us safer? Not from our government, which has done little to earn our trust over the years, especially when it comes to law enforcement. And not from terrorists, either. If *they've* been cowed, it's because we went after bin Laden and his minions with specific, extreme, and righteous prejudice. It's because of regular people who took the terrorists down over Pennsylvania instead of the White House, and who wrestled shoe bomber Richard Reid onto the floor at 30,000 feet. It's because, as a nation and as individuals, we showed that we would fight for a way of life that values freedom and privacy.

How wrong, then, that we've dealt away some of our freedom and privacy for a promise of safety and security. To be sure, today's America is not [writer Jeremy] Bentham's *Panopticon* [which discusses a theme for improving prison discipline and establish an equitable legal system] or Orwell's dystopia [*1984*] (or even [Fidel] Castro's). It's not even solely a product of the September attacks, which merely hurried along trends that were already well under way. But in making the freedom-for-safety swap, we haven't just dishonored the dead of 9/11. We've helped something else die too.

"*[Our civil liberties] should be curtailed, to the extent that the benefits in greater security outweigh the costs in reduced liberty.*"

Some Curtailment of Civil Liberties Is Necessary to Enhance National Security

Richard A. Posner

In the following viewpoint, Richard A. Posner contends that in times of crisis nations must weigh public-safety concerns against the protection of civil liberties. According to Posner, the U.S. Constitution allows for flexible interpretations of constitutional provisions for civil liberties, permitting legislators and judges the latitude to constrain freedom when doing so results in more good than harm. The September 11, 2001, terrorist attacks clearly illustrate the need for improving security at the expense of some civil liberties, he contends. Posner is a judge of the U.S. Court of Appeals for the Seventh Circuit and a senior lecturer at the University of Chicago Law School.

As you read, consider the following questions:
1. Why does the author believe that the September 11, 2001, terrorist attacks mandate a restriction of civil liberties?
2. What historical examples does Posner provide to illustrate how the United States has frequently underestimated the dangers to national security?
3. What war is America fighting that Posner thinks illustrates a bad tradeoff between civil liberties and public safety?

In the wake of the September 11, 2001, terrorist attacks have come many proposals for tightening security; some measures to that end have already been taken. Civil libertarians are troubled. They fear that concerns about national security will lead to an erosion of civil liberties. They offer historical examples of supposed overreactions to threats to national security. They treat our existing civil liberties— freedom of the press, protections of privacy and of the rights of criminal suspects, and the rest—as sacrosanct, insisting that the battle against international terrorism accommodate itself to them.

Weighing Competing Interests

I consider this a profoundly mistaken approach to the question of balancing liberty and security. The basic mistake is the prioritizing of liberty. It is a mistake about law and a mistake about history. Let me begin with law. What we take to be our civil liberties—for example, immunity from arrest except upon probable cause to believe we've committed a crime, and from prosecution for violating a criminal statute enacted after we committed the act that violates it—were made legal rights by the Constitution and other enactments. The other enactments can be changed relatively easily, by amendatory legislation. Amending the Constitution is much more difficult. In recognition of this the Framers left most of the constitutional provisions that confer rights pretty vague. The courts have made them definite.

Concretely, the scope of these rights has been determined, through an interaction of constitutional text and subsequent judicial interpretation, by a weighing of competing interests. I'll call them the public-safety interest and the liberty interest. Neither, in my view, has priority. They are both important, and their relative importance changes from time to time and from situation to situation. The safer the nation feels, the more weight judges will be willing to give to the liberty interest. The greater the threat that an activity poses to the nation's safety, the stronger will the grounds seem for seeking to repress that activity even at some cost to liberty. This fluid approach is only common sense.

If it is true, therefore, as it appears to be at this writing, that the events of September 11 have revealed the United States to be in much greater jeopardy from international terrorism than had previously been believed—have revealed it to be threatened by a diffuse, shadowy enemy that must be fought with police measures as well as military force—it stands to reason that our civil liberties will be curtailed. They should be curtailed, to the extent that the benefits in greater security outweigh the costs in reduced liberty. All that can reasonably be asked of the responsible legislative and judicial officials is that they weigh the costs as carefully as the benefits.

Underestimating Threats to Security

It will be argued that the lesson of history is that officials habitually exaggerate dangers to the nation's security. But the lesson of history is the opposite. It is because officials have repeatedly and disastrously underestimated these dangers that our history is as violent as it is. Consider such underestimated dangers as that of secession, which led to the Civil War; of a Japanese attack on the United States, which led to the disaster at Pearl Harbor; of Soviet espionage in the 1940s, which accelerated the Soviet Union's acquisition of nuclear weapons and emboldened Stalin to encourage North Korea's invasion of South Korea; of the installation of Soviet missiles in Cuba, which precipitated the Cuban missile crisis; of political assassinations and outbreaks of urban violence in the 1960s; of the Tet Offensive of 1968; of the Iranian revolution of 1979 and the subsequent taking of American diplomats as hostages; and, for that matter, of the events of September 11.

It is true that when we are surprised and hurt, we tend to overreact—but only with the benefit of hindsight can a reaction be separated into its proper and excess layers. In hindsight we know that interning Japanese Americans did not shorten World War II. But was this known at the time? If not, shouldn't the Army have erred on the side of caution, as it did? Even today we cannot say with any assurance that Abraham Lincoln was wrong to suspend habeas corpus during the Civil War, as he did on several occasions, even though the Constitution is clear that only Congress can suspend this right. (Another of Lincoln's wartime measures, the Emancipation Proclamation, may also have been unconstitutional.) But Lincoln would have been wrong to cancel the 1864 presidential election, as some urged: by November of 1864 the North was close to victory, and canceling the election would have created a more dangerous precedent than the wartime suspension of habeas corpus. This last example shows that civil liberties remain part of the balance even in the most dangerous of times, and even though their relative weight must then be less.

Checks and Balances Keep Violations at Bay

A year after 9/11, it's worth engaging in a cautious celebration of the resilience of our constitutional checks and balances. So far, in the face of great stress, the system has worked relatively well. The executive branch tried to increase its own authority across the board, but the courts and Congress are insisting on a more reasoned balance between liberty and security. Of all of the lessons about America's strength that have emerged since the attacks, this is one of the most reassuring.

Jeffrey Rosen, *Washington Post*, September 23–29, 2002.

Lincoln's unconstitutional acts during the Civil War show that even legality must sometimes be sacrificed for other values. We are a nation under law, but first we are a nation. I want to emphasize something else, however: the malleability of law, its pragmatic rather than dogmatic character. The law is not absolute, and the slogan *"Fiat iustitia rat caelum"* ("Let justice be done though the heavens fall") is dangerous nonsense. The law is a human creation rather than a divine gift, a tool of government rather than a mandarin mystery. It is an instrument for promoting social welfare, and as the conditions essential to that welfare change, so must it change.

Reprioritizing America's Wars

Civil libertarians today are missing something else—the opportunity to challenge other public-safety concerns that impair civil liberties. I have particularly in mind the war on drugs. The sale of illegal drugs is a "victimless" crime in the special but important sense that it is a consensual activity.

Usually there is no complaining witness, so in order to bring the criminals to justice the police have to rely heavily on paid informants (often highly paid and often highly unsavory), undercover agents, wiretaps and other forms of electronic surveillance, elaborate sting operations, the infiltration of suspect organizations, random searches, the monitoring of airports and highways, the "profiling" of likely suspects on the basis of ethnic or racial identity or national origin, compulsory drug tests, and other intrusive methods that put pressure on civil liberties. The war on drugs has been a big flop; moreover, in light of what September 11 has taught us about the gravity of the terrorist threat to the United States, it becomes hard to take entirely seriously the threat to the nation that drug use is said to pose. Perhaps it is time to redirect law-enforcement resources from the investigation and apprehension of drug dealers to the investigation and apprehension of international terrorists. By doing so we may be able to minimize the net decrease in our civil liberties that the events of September 11 have made inevitable.

"How can we be putting all this work into appearances when appearances bear no necessary relation to intent?"

Ethnic Profiling Is Ineffective and Unfair

Patricia J. Williams

Law professor Patricia J. Williams asserts in the following viewpoint that ethnic profiling—the practice of identifying suspects based on their physical appearance—violates civil liberties and will ultimately prove ineffective at fighting terrorism. She contends that innocent people have been killed and guilty ones allowed to go free because officials based their decisions on the suspects' physical characteristics. Since a person's appearance does not always convey his or her intention of committing a wrongful act, ethnic profiling will ultimately fail to identify terrorists, she claims. Moreover, Williams maintains, clever terrorists will always find ways to disguise themselves in order to circumvent ethnic profiling.

As you read, consider the following questions:
1. According to Williams, which individuals are most often profiled as drug couriers?
2. Why was Richard Reid allowed to board a commercial aircraft despite his suspicious looks, as reported by the author?
3. What CIA incident in Afghanistan does Williams use to bolster her argument that ethnic profiling is wrong?

Patricia J. Williams, "Better Safe . . . ?," *The Nation*, vol. 274, March 11, 2002, p. 9. Copyright © 2002 by The Nation Company, Inc. Reproduced by permission.

In my last column, I called the expansion of profiling that has occurred since the [September 11, 2001, terrorist attacks] "equal opportunity." I meant it ironically, but a surprising number of people took me literally. So I want to make clear that I don't consider this upgraded frisking any kind of opportunity, nor do I think that its expansion is really the same as equality. I am also aware, as was pointed out to me, that there are people in the world who might appreciate a good cavity search, confident that this is all for their benefit. And while I understand that we have all become subject to "nothing more than" the same ministrations that visitors to maximum security prisoners go through, the fact that some think this is the best of all possible worlds strikes me as fatuous.

An Unprecedented Investment in a Heavily Patrolled World

The billions of dollars currently being pumped into police and surveillance budgets represent an unprecedented investment in a heavily patrolled world. Such an extraordinary buildup will inevitably exacerbate questions about the limits of state force; it will require the greatest vigilance to prevent our turning into not just a police state but one big global military base. Specific categories of us will probably continue to bear a special burden—black women in airports are, according to some figures, searched more than anyone else because I, as Typical Black Everywoman, meet the description of a drug courier better than you—as in You, profiled *Nation* reader and Typical Ungendered White Person.

Blacks and Latinos are the profiled shape of the "war on drugs," even though the majority of actual drug abusers are young white people like [Florida] Governor Jeb Bush's poor daughter, Noelle. The "war on terror" promises to be even more sweeping. For the time being, our new international, militarized police force has increased its scrutiny, from black women in airports and black men in cars, to include Middle Eastern men anywhere, Asian people who look vaguely Filipino, as well as ample Minnesota housewives actually armed with sets of silver fondue forks.

Is this better or worse? I think it's a misuse of data, often creating a false sense of security. The kind of profiling that seems to inform the majority of stops and searches is usually based on statistical relations so vague as to be useless. Such profiling, premised on diffuse probabilities about looks and dress, ethnicity or nationality, class or educational status, begs for more analysis. Otherwise it can be defeated on the one hand by guards and gatekeepers whose interpretation of looks or class status is skewed by selective and subjective prejudice and on the other hand by travelers committed to the art of disguise.

The attacks on the Pentagon and the World Trade Center were carried out by deeply rational and well-trained operatives whose tactics defied easy profiling. They looked—and were—well educated; they dressed professionally. The fact that the FBI actually had information that some of them had been involved in terrorist networks counted less in the real world than that they looked good. After all, it is true that in a very large sense sleek, well-dressed professionals commit fewer crimes than the hungry, grumpy lower classes. I have this painful recurring dream of the security guards at Logan [airport] on September 11, carelessly waving all eighteen [terrorists] through, while strip searching long lines of black women having bad hair days.

Not Defined by Biology

It does make sense to take a second look at Muslims if you are worried about Muslim terrorists. The problem with racial profiling, however, is that Islam is not defined by biology. There are millions of Muslims with skin whiter than [President] George W. Bush's. O.K., so why don't we just scrutinize "Middle Easternlooking people"? Again there is a problem. The Middle East is a place, and it is home to a highly diverse population.

Guy Harrison, *Free Inquiry*, Summer 2002.

I worry that we're doing the same thing with shoes: Richard Reid was able to board an airplane because he played against the expectation embedded in profiles. He looked odd enough to have been stopped and questioned, but ultimately looks had little to do with what made him dangerous. Although they were suspicious, security officials did not discover his criminal record, surely better evidence of his propensities than whether he wore a ponytail. He was finally allowed on board; he was a British citizen, and British citizens were not the subject of any profile. They searched his bag but not his shoes, because shoes were not at that point the subject of any profile. Now that we know thick-soled sneakers can be turned into weapons of mass destruction, airports spend a lot of time removing and examining them. It's likely to catch copycats, I suppose, which is not a problem to be ignored, but does anyone really believe that the Al Qaeda [terrorist network] would use shoes again? In other words, while there is, after Richard Reid, a marginal relation between shoes and bombs, the actual odds of it ever happening precisely like that again are slim to nonexistent. Indeed, what distinguishes professional operatives who calculatedly sow terror is that they take the time to play against type.

The Problem with Appearances

So I worry when I hear about plans to expand profiling as we now seem to practice it. I worry when I hear about plans to have our thumb prints taken, our irises scanned, our DNA plotted. How can we be putting all this work into appearances when appearances bear no necessary relation to intent? The risk of this is not just one of diminished dignity or privacy.

The problem ought to have been made clear to us in the wake of "accidents" like [the police shooting of black man] Amadou Diallo [who turned out to be innocent]. The problem ought to be apparent in recent news stories about the CIA having flown an unmanned surveillance craft over a street in Afghanistan. It had a night vision camera on it that caught in its scope a group of men conversing who fit a profile because one of their number was unusually tall, as is Osama bin Laden. After some consultation at the remote site where the CIA officers and their telemonitors were located, the CIA decided to bomb the group. The men were killed, but as of this writing, the CIA admits it still doesn't know who the men were. Civilians on the ground claimed that the men were townspeople scavenging for scrap metal.

This death by actuary. This profiled guilt. This trial by

night vision drone. Our superlative technology permits us to listen, scan, survey and X-ray anybody and everybody in the world. But a sea of data alone won't help us if there is no higher wisdom in the final analysis. Good "intelligence" means more than eyes and ears—there must be a heart and a brain, or we will never achieve the global stability we all so desperately desire.

"Common sense demands the use of profiling if the United States is going to have any chance to prevent or at least reduce the number of terrorist atrocities in the future."

Ethnic Profiling Is Necessary to Prevent Terrorism

Bruce J. Terris

Attorney Bruce J. Terris contends in the following viewpoint that ethnic profiling can help protect Americans from future terrorist attacks. In Israel, Terris claims, officials interrogate individuals most likely to commit terrorist attacks—Arabs. He claims that implementing such a strategy in the United States would be far preferable to other procedures currently being used in U.S. airports, such as arbitrarily choosing those who will be interrogated, which is unlikely to catch real terrorists. Terris argues that government and media vigilance could guarantee that ethnic profiling would not violate anyone's civil liberties.

As you read, consider the following questions:
1. How do the police use profiling, according to Terris?
2. In the author's opinion, why do Ben Gurion airport security procedures take so little time?
3. In addition to flying airplanes into buildings, what other kinds of terrorist attacks are terrorism experts worried about, as reported by Terris?

Bruce J. Terris, "Common Sense in Profiling," *Midstream*, vol. 48, February/March 2002, pp. 11–12. Copyright © 2002 by Theodor Herzl Foundation. Reproduced by permission.

A few days after [the September 11, 2001, terrorist attacks on America], passengers or pilots on several flights refused to fly when they saw several Arabs about to board the planes. They were roundly condemned by officialdom and the press. But they were right. They were using common sense. They were simply doing basic "profiling," determining that future terrorist actions were also likely to be carried out by Arab males.

I am not going to discuss court decisions that have considered the profiling of minorities. I am not doing so because I have faith in American courts interpreting the Constitution consistent with common sense. And, as I will discuss, common sense demands the use of profiling if the United States is going to have any chance to prevent or at least reduce the number of terrorist atrocities in the future.

Commonsense Profiling

The police use profiling as a matter of course. Let me give an example. If eyewitnesses describe bank robbers as being Arabs, the police will, of course, in looking for the criminals, naturally concentrate their attention on Arabs. However, since the eyewitnesses may be wrong, competent policemen will not devote all their resources to investigating Arabs. But they will proportionally stop far more Arabs at roadblocks than non-Arabs, look for likely criminals in the Arab community, and describe the likely criminals as Arabs to the media so that the public can be alerted to help find them.

I assume that no one would object to this profiling, since it is based on concrete evidence that the bank robbers were probably Arabs. However, the evidence is just as strong that future terrorist attacks are likely to be committed by Arabs. All nineteen of the hijackers who crashed the four planes on September 11th were Arabs. The suspects who have since been picked up by the FBI are entirely or at least mostly Arabs. The terrorist attacks against Americans, which cost hundreds of lives during the last decade in Lebanon, Saudi Arabia, Kenya, Tanzania, and Yemen, have all been carried out by Arabs. The Arab terrorist organization run by Osama bin Laden has openly stated that it intends to continue with its terrorism against the United States. One has to be politically correct to the point of blindness not to believe that future attacks are likely to be carried out by Arabs.

This, of course, does not mean that other sources should be ignored. It is possible that Arabs will recruit non-Arabs to do their dirty work, that non-Arab terrorist organizations in places like Spain and South America will be encouraged by the events of September 11th to commit terrorism in the United States, or that home-grown ideologues like Timothy McVeigh [who bombed the Alfred P. Murrah Federal Building in Oklahoma City in 1995] or crackpots will engage in terrorism. But these possibilities are far less likely or are at least far less likely to have the incredible results of September 11th.

The Israel Example

The experience of Israel in combating terrorism shows what needs to be done in this country. Israel has been the number one target of Arab terrorists for decades, but no Israeli plane has ever been hijacked, and no other terrorist acts have ever resulted in anything close to the loss of life that occurred on September 11th. The reason customarily given for this success is the tight security in Ben Gurion airport.

I have flown out of Ben Gurion more than 150 times in the last 20 years. The Israeli success does not come from using scanners or asking the usual questions—did you pack this bag yourself, and has it been under your control since you packed it? Instead, the heart of the Israeli system is that they profile. They concentrate their attention on the people that they believe are likely to be most dangerous.

The Israelis use intelligent and well-trained security to question all passengers, not sales representatives who handle check-in at airline counters. Based on profiling, some passengers are questioned for only a couple of minutes. Others, who appear more suspicious, may be questioned for 15 to 30 minutes. A few have their hand- and checked-luggage searched from top to bottom.

The Israeli criteria for profiling have not, for obvious reasons, been published. But it is obvious, from my watching the proceedings in Ben Gurion so many times, that Israelis other than Arabs are questioned for only a couple of minutes, and their luggage is rarely checked. A small number of Americans and Europeans, who satisfy some criteria for suspicion, are questioned longer, and a very few have their hand-luggage searched. In contrast, virtually all Arabs are thoroughly questioned and their luggage carefully gone through.

FIND THE TERRORIST
(No Profiling Allowed)

Gorrell. © 2002 by Bob Gorrell. Reprinted by permission.

Several times, *The Washington Post* has reported that the United States could never adopt the Israeli approach, because passengers in Israel are delayed for 45 minutes or more going through security and the delay would be worse in the busy airports of the United States. However, it has never taken me more than 10 minutes to go through security at Ben Gurion, including the time waiting to be questioned. I have seen very few other passengers waiting for longer than 10 or 15 minutes. The few exceptions are passengers who fall within the suspect categories. The process takes so little time, because the Israelis have enough security personnel to handle the number of passengers boarding the particular plane and the operation is efficiently organized. There is no reason why the United States cannot run just as efficient and effective operations if it chooses to do so.

In comparison, not long ago I took a flight from Reagan National Airport to Newark to Tel Aviv. On the domestic flight to Newark, my checked-luggage was run through a scanner, but only because I was flying to Israel. The checked-luggage of none of the other passengers was scanned. Hand-luggage belonging to only two of the approximately 50 passengers was examined by security personnel. The choice was made arbitrarily, by computer. As it happened, I was chosen. So after 150 flights to and from Israel and the United States, my hand-luggage was finally searched, not at Ben Gurion but in Washington, D.C. I would have had no objection, except that I know that such arbitrary decision-making is totally ineffective to guard against terrorists.

In contrast, before the flight from Newark to Tel Aviv, the hand-luggage of every passenger was carefully checked, and a wand and pat-down were used on the person of every passenger. This took almost an hour. This system is admirably effective. However, this is not done on domestic flights, like the ones that were used to crash planes into the World Trade Center, and it is probably not going to continue, even for most international flights, in view of the cost and delay.

Existing luggage scanners, even the new improved varieties, cannot detect every weapon, every explosive material, and every other dangerous object. Yet, it is obvious that American airports are not going to search carefully the luggage and person of every passenger. If every piece of luggage and every passenger were carefully searched, the cost would be astronomical and the delay prohibitive. The only alternatives are to check nobody, to check a few passengers arbitrarily, or to attempt to choose rationally the passengers who present the greatest danger.

Rational Profiling Criteria

In light of the events of September 11th, we can obviously not afford to check nobody. If we check passengers arbitrarily, we will waste precious resources checking blacks, Hispanics, and Norwegians, even though experience tells us that they are extremely unlikely to be hijackers. We will check 80-year-old women and 8-year-old children. It would be pure luck if we happened to check the actual terrorists. On the other hand, if experts establish rational profiling criteria, we can concentrate our efforts on the categories of passengers likely to be dangerous.

The issue of profiling does not apply only to airplane flights. Terrorism experts warn that future terrorist attacks may involve trucks loaded with explosives, as in the attacks in Kenya and Tanzania. As a result, for one day, the police checked every truck going through the Baltimore Harbor Tunnel. When massive traffic jams developed, the effort was abandoned. Now, only spot checks are being made. But profiling is not being done to concentrate on the truck drivers likely to pose the greatest danger. Similarly, vehicles crossing the border from Canada are either being checked carefully, causing massive lines, or are not being checked at all.

It is argued that no government actions in the United States should be based on ethnicity, or race, or religion. However, . . . law enforcement agencies regularly profile in order to solve crimes, even though they may not use this term. The terrorist danger now facing the United States is far more serious than any bank robbery or other criminal acts against which profiling is now being used.

No doubt, profiling can be abused. It can be used for crimes that are not serious enough to justify the use of ethnic or racial criteria. It can be used when its basis is simple bigotry. But virtually any law enforcement technique that is appropriate for some situations can be used illegally or immorally in other situations. The only remedy for such abuse is constant vigilance by higher government officials, the media, and the public to assure that profiling is only used when it is appropriate to do so. The danger from terrorism in the United States is now so grave and so clear that the need for profiling easily satisfies any such standard.

Political correctness cannot be allowed to divert this country away from targeting in airports and other dangerous situations the people most likely to be terrorists. We should not be wasting time, and effort, and money checking people who almost certainly are not dangerous, just so we can pretend that we are treating all people alike. Should we really check carefully 80-year-old black grandmothers, so we can say that we are not singling out 25-year-old Arabs? The answer is so obvious that it is only common sense.

"That [the federal government] should be able to [track Americans' habits] better and more efficiently is . . . a prospect to be dreaded."

National ID Cards Would Threaten Civil Liberties

John Derbyshire

Following the September 11, 2001, terrorist attacks on America, many people advocated instituting a system in which every U.S. citizen would be required to carry a national ID card. John Derbyshire argues in the following viewpoint that a mandatory national ID card would destroy the freedoms that define America, a nation in which people can move freely and engage in private interactions with others without government interference. According to Derbyshire, such a card—which would contain the holder's name, address, photo, and fingerprint—would not help fight terrorism. In fact, in Derbyshire's opinion, real terrorists would continue to evade detection while average Americans' lives would be scrutinized by unscrupulous government officials. John Derbyshire is a columnist for the *National Review*.

As you read, consider the following questions:

1. How often is the Immigration and Naturalization Service database wrong, according to Derbyshire?
2. What example does the author provide to illustrate how government workers can violate the public's trust?
3. According to the author, how did former president Ronald Reagan react after getting shot by a "lunatic"?

John Derbyshire, "Your Papers, Please: Against a National ID Card," *National Review*, vol. 53, November 5, 2001. Copyright © 2001 by National Review, Inc. Reproduced by permission.

In the present climate of concern about security, we have been hearing renewed calls for a national identity card. Larry Ellison, the CEO of Oracle Corp., which sells software for managing large databases, had a piece in the *Wall Street Journal*: "Digital IDs Can Help Prevent Terrorism." Ellison does not go into much detail about how a national ID card might actually prevent terrorism; in fact he leaves one with the impression that terrorists who were careful to keep their noses clean while in the U.S.A. would go undetected anyway.

A few days later, Alan Dershowitz, the notorious professor and lawyer, chimed in with an op-ed in the *New York Times*: "Why Fear National ID Cards?" Dershowitz imagines a minimal system: "The only information the card need contain is name, address, photo and [finger]print." Such a system would, he argues, actually enhance civil liberties by "reducing the need for racial and ethnic stereotyping." It is encouraging to know that the professor acknowledges such a need; though since, by the time the ID card has been requested and presented, the profiling has already occurred, it is hard to see how the card would help.

Both writers make the point that all sorts of databases already exist, full of information about our incomes, movements, and private lives. A national ID-card system would simply make more efficient and useful what already exists in a chaotic and diffuse form. Ellison: "All these separate databases make it difficult for one agency to know about and apprehend someone wanted by another agency." Dershowitz: "[The card] would reduce the likelihood that someone could, intentionally or not, get lost in the cracks of multiple bureaucracies."

A Prospect to Be Dreaded

Well, yes. Reading things like that, I feel that I am looking at one of those optical tricks—like the stack of cubes that seem to be ascending and lit from below, until you blink and perceive them as descending and lit from above. What Ellison and Dershowitz deplore—the possibility that an individual can lurk quietly in the interstices of our numerous national databases—seems to me a guarantor of individual liberty in the United States. It is sufficiently disturbing that the federal government can, by sorting through a pile of conflicting and unreliable data, track my movements and habits with modest accuracy. That they should be able to do this better and more efficiently is, it seems to me, a prospect to be dreaded.

There are other problems with a national ID-card database. There is the issue of data quality, for example. A study by the (libertarian) Cato Institute in 1995 showed that large databases owned by the federal government had high error rates: 5 to 20 percent for the Social Security Administration, and 10 to 20 percent for the IRS. The Immigration and Naturalization Service (INS) database, they found, was unreliable 28 percent of the time; people's first and last names were routinely in the wrong order, and misspellings were "rampant."

The National ID Card: Selling America's Soul

Orwellian fears of bureaucratic snooping fuel much of [the resistance to a national ID card], but not all of it. There's a positive preference at work as well: for fluidity over stability, for dynamism over lamination. In America to be ID'd— sorted, tagged, and permanently filed—is to lose a bit of one's soul. To die a little.

Walter Kirn, *Atlantic Monthly*, May 2002.

And then there is the matter of abuse. Because of the attacks on our country, we are currently in a collectivist frame of mind, with the percentage of Americans who say they trust the federal government to do the right thing "nearly always" or "most of the time" currently at 64—twice the level of a year ago. I hope and believe that the sober style of the new administration has also made some contribution to this high level of trust. We must remember, though, that a national ID database, once established, would be available to all future administrations. It is hard to imagine the George W. Bush people allowing low-level staffers to riffle through FBI files, or siccing the IRS on the president's personal enemies: yet exactly these things happened in previous years. Both of our editorialists are blithe about the possibility of abuse. Dershowitz: "The fear of an intrusive government can be addressed by setting criteria for any official who demands to see the card." Ellison: "Fourth Amendment protections against unreasonable search and seizure would govern access . . . The 'probable cause' standard will still have to be met."

Compare the following, taken pretty much at random from the immense literature on government abuse of power and disregard of the law and the Constitution in the 1990s: "In August 1993 the IRS revealed that 369 of its employees in one regional office had been investigated for browsing through the returns of friends, relatives, celebrities and others" (from *Feeling Your Pain* by James Bovard).

The cheerful confidence of Dershowitz and Ellison in the efficacy of "criteria" and "probable cause" as means of restraining government workers who are psychotic, venal, overzealous, or just inquisitive about the data in their charge, contrasts rather starkly with what we know about the actual behavior of actual bureaucrats when entrusted with our secrets, especially when, as apparently is fated to happen every so often, our government falls into the hands of liars and thieves.

A Fool's Paradise?

And yet many Americans will feel that there is no choice. We have, they will say, been living in a fool's paradise: a quaint but hopelessly outdated notion of a country in which people can move freely without asking leave of anyone, can live lives free of interference by government busybodies, can engage in private transactions among themselves without any restraints other than those necessary to protect the weak from the strong. To prevent us from being ravaged by foreign evildoers like [terrorist] Osama bin Laden, we must submit to a more "European" style of life, with more supervision by the authorities.

I do not accept this. A few elementary precautions and a rational immigration policy would do a great deal to prevent the repetition of a [September 11, 2001, terrorist attack]–type horror. A swift and vigorous response to all attacks on Americans—either civilians or troops, either at home or abroad—would work wonders in the way of deterrence. Even with all that, however, there is no perfect security; the odd lunatic or terrorist will always slip through the net. Then hundreds of us—or, in the rarest case, thousands of us—will be killed or maimed. There is a limit to what we can do to prevent this, short of instituting a system of permanent surveillance of all citizens and visitors, monitored by a vast army of snoopers.

In this, as in so many other things, [former president] Ronald Reagan set the example. He did not waver in his support for Second Amendment [gun ownership] rights even when he himself was shot by a lunatic, regarding such an occurrence as part of the price for living in a free society. In the same spirit, when the subject of a national ID card, as an aid to controlling illegal immigration, was raised during a cabinet meeting, Reagan dismissed it with the sardonic remark: "Maybe we should just brand all babies." (This from Martin Anderson's book *Revolution*.) In the present climate, one hesitates to tell that story, for fear the idea might be taken up in all seriousness and appear a few days later as a *New York Times* editorial.

| *"A high-tech, hard-to-forge driver's license could become a national E-ZPass, a way for a law-abiding citizen to move faster through the roadblocks of post-9/11 life."*

National ID Cards Would Help Fight Terrorism

Margaret Carlson

The September 11, 2001, terrorist attacks on America generated renewed calls for a system in which every U.S. citizen would be required to carry a national ID card. Margaret Carlson contends in the following viewpoint that a national ID card would enable government officials to make better use of the widely dispersed data it keeps on all residents. Carlson believes that unlike credit card companies and other commercial interests, who exploit personal information for private gain, the government can be trusted to use such data appropriately. She maintains that issuing a national ID card—which would include each U.S. resident's name, address, photo, and finger- or palm print—would be superior to other efforts to combat terrorism, such as ethnic profiling and airport passenger searches. Carlson is a writer for *Time* magazine.

As you read, consider the following questions:

1. What happened to U.S. representative John Dingell that convinced Carlson that America needs a national ID card?
2. As reported by the author, what is Richard Durbin's plan for implementing a national ID card?
3. What percentage of Americans support a national ID card, according to Carlson?

After representative John Dingell was asked to drop his pants at Washington's National Airport last week [in January 2002], some people felt safer. Others, like me, decided that we'd lost our collective minds. A near strip search of a 75-year-old Congressman whose artificial hip has set off a metal detector—while suspected al-Qaeda [terrorist network] operative Richard Reid slips onto a Paris-to-Miami flight with a bomb in his shoe—isn't making us safer. It's making us ridiculous for entrusting our security to an unskilled police force that must make split-second decisions on the basis of incomplete data.

Incidents like this—and airport waits longer than the flight itself—have pushed me into the camp of the national ID card. Yes, a tamperproof ID smacks of Big Brother and Nazis intoning "Your papers, please," but the Federal Government already holds a trove of data on each of us. And it's less likely to mess up or misuse it than the credit-card companies or the Internet fraudsters, who have just as much data if not more. (Two years ago, for a *Time* article, I ordered dinner for 30 entirely online, and I am still plagued by vendors who know I like my wine French and my ham honey-baked.)

The idea of a national ID card leaped into the headlines just after [the September 11, 2001, terrorist attacks]. Oracle chairman Larry Ellison offered to donate the pertinent software. Ellison went to see Attorney General John Ashcroft, who was noncommittal despite his obvious enthusiasm for expanding government powers into other areas that trouble civil libertarians.

Enter Richard Durbin. In concert with the American Association of Motor Vehicle Administrators (yes, the dreaded DMVs have their own trade group), the Illinois Senator is proposing legislation that would create a uniform standard for the country's 200 million state-administered driver's licenses. Durbin noticed that the driver's license has become "the most widely used personal ID in the country. If you can produce one, we assume you're legitimate," he says. At present, nearly anyone can get a license; 13 of the 19 hijackers did. Having those licenses "gave the terrorists cover to mingle in American society without being detected."

Since we're using the driver's license as a de facto national

ID, Durbin argues, let's make it more reliable. As it stands, the chief requirement is that one knows how to drive. This is fine if the only intent is to ensure that someone behind the wheel has mastered turn signals, but it shouldn't be sufficient to get someone into a federal building, the Olympics or an airplane. All a terrorist needs to do is shop around for a lax state (Florida still doesn't require proof of permanent residency) or resort to a forger with a glue gun and laminator.

Deterring Identity Theft

I . . . see a national ID card as an additional deterrent to yet another escalating problem plaguing our country—identity theft. A card that really proves you are you would simplify transactions and prevent future applications from being hindered by suspicion. . . . No longer will double or triple proofs of identity be requested for simple things like check cashing or serious tasks such as global travel.

David Bursky, *Electronic Design*, September 16, 2002.

A high-tech, hard-to-forge driver's license could become a national E-ZPass, a way for a law-abiding citizen to move faster through the roadblocks of post-9/11 life. It's no digitalized Supercard, but the states would have uniform standards, using bar codes and biometrics (a unique characteristic, like a palm print) and could cross-check and get information from other law-enforcement agencies. Polls show 70% of Americans support an even more stringent ID. But Japanese-American members of Congress and Transportation Secretary Norman Mineta are keenly sensitive to anything that might single out one nationality. Yet an ID card offers prospects of less profiling. By accurately identifying those who are in the U.S. legally and not on a terrorist watch list, the card would reduce the temptation to go after random members of specific groups.

It is not ideal to leave a national problem to the states, but because of the general squeamishness about federal "papers" in the Congress, Durbin's proposal—congressional oversight of state DMVs—may be the best way to go. And if the government doesn't act, corporations will. Delta and American Airlines already provide separate lines for premium passengers; Heathrow Airport in London [England] has an iris scan for people who have registered their eyeballs. An airline-industry association is at work on a Trusted Traveler card. Do we really want frequent-flyer status to be the basis for security decisions, or more plastic cards joining the too many we already have?

This ID would require one virtual strip search instead of many real ones. Durbin says the card would remove the anonymity of a [terrorist like] Mohamed Atta but not the privacy of others. With a card, Dingell could have confirmed his identity (though he made a point of not pulling rank). With the presumption that he wasn't a terrorist, a once-over with a wand—with his pants on—would have lent credence to his claim that he possessed an artificial hip, not a gun. The Durbin card would at least let us travel with our clothes on.

Periodical Bibliography

The following articles have been selected to supplement the diverse views presented in this chapter.

David M. Brown — "The Danger of National Identification," *Ideas on Liberty*, October 2002.

David Bursky — "National ID Card: The Ultimate Security Measure," *Electronic Design*, September 26, 2002.

CQ Researcher — "Civil Liberties in Wartime," December 14, 2001.

DARPA — "Total Information Awareness (TIA) System" www.darpa.mil.

Valerie Demmer — "Civil Liberties and Homeland Security," *Humanist*, January/February 2002.

David Harrison — "From Racial to Religious Profiling," *Free Inquiry*, Summer 2002.

Nat Hentoff — "We'll All Be Under Surveillance," *Nation*, December 6, 2002.

Walter Kirn — "The Mother of Reinvention: The Real Reason Americans Detest the Idea of a National ID Card," *Atlantic Monthly*, May 2002.

Charles Krauthammer — "The Case for Profiling: Why Random Searches of Airline Travelers Are a Useless Charade," *Time*, March 18, 2002.

Marshall Lewin — "Big Brother's Invasive Gaze," *America's 1st Freedom*, April 2002.

David Moberg — "Every Breath You Take: Will the Feds Be Watching You?" *In These Times*, October 29, 2001.

Newsday — "In Reality, 'Big Brother' Soon May Be Watching You," December 1, 2002.

Jeffrey Rosen — "A Lesson in Liberties," *Washington Post*, September 23–29, 2002.

Peter H. Schuck — "A Case for Profiling," *American Lawyer*, January 2002.

David Tell — "Civil Hysteria," *Weekly Standard*, July 29, 2002.

For Further Discussion

Chapter 1

1. Michael L. Rothschild contends that the steady stream of news stories about the threat of terrorist attacks has instilled in Americans an exaggerated sense of personal danger. Do Rothschild's criticisms of the media cause you to question George J. Tenet's argument that terrorism is a serious threat to national security? Or, does Tenet provide enough evidence to convince you of such a threat? Quote both authors while constructing your answer.

2. Antony T. Sullivan claims that Western critics of Islam have erroneously portrayed Islam as an enemy of the West. In contrast to their views, Sullivan contends that Islam is a religion of compassion and mercy. Antony Flew, on the other hand, argues that Islam encourages adherents to convert the entire world to Islam. What factors might encourage critics to unquestionably condemn Islam? Why might supporters come to Islam's defense without equivocation? After reading both viewpoints, what middle-of-the-road view of Islam might be advocated?

3. Steve Bonta maintains that biological weapons could not be used effectively against a modern society that has good sanitation and advanced medicine. Review the biological weapons dangers discussed by Veronique de Rugy and Charles V. Peña. In your opinion, would the modern safeguards described by Bonta be sufficient to contain the threat? Please explain.

Chapter 2

1. Paul Wolfowitz argues that the United States should spend whatever is necessary on defense to protect national security. Paul Isaacs contends that out-of-control defense spending will not make America safer. In your opinion, is it better to establish a bigger military than may prove necessary, just in case, or would it be preferable to keep defense spending to a minimum so that money could be used for other government programs, such as those that help the poor? Please explain your answer.

2. Jim Garamone lists countless nations that have or are developing weapons of mass destruction to support his argument that America needs a missile defense system. David Wright and Theodore Postol describe several countermeasures that hostile nations could use to defeat such a system to support their contention that missile defense is technologically infeasible. After analyzing the evidence provided in both viewpoints, which au-

thor(s) do you find more persuasive? Cite from the texts to develop your answer.

3. George W. Bush claims that America must confront the threat posed by Iran, Iraq, and North Korea because these nations are developing weapons of mass destruction that they could provide to terrorists to use against the United States. Llewellyn D. Howell disagrees, claiming that these nations are not working in concert to undermine the United States. In fact, he argues, to focus on them is to ignore the real threat to national security: terrorist groups such as al-Qaeda. Examine the information that both authors provide about Iran, Iraq, and North Korea. In your opinion, which author's use of facts is more persuasive?

Chapter 3

1. Stephen Cox contends that the United States should kill terrorists who threaten America's security as a way of deterring other terrorists. However, Stephen G. Cary argues that killing terrorists will only make other terrorists and potential terrorists angrier, thus breeding more terrorism. In your opinion, which author is more convincing? Please explain, citing from the texts.

2. Michael J. Glennon maintains that laws forbidding the use of force except in self-defense, as outlined in the UN Charter, are antiquated and can be legitimately ignored. In contrast, Richard Falk asserts that such laws are still binding, making it wrong to use preemptive force. Which author uses the UN Charter most persuasively to bolster his argument? Explain.

3. George W. Bush argues in favor of the creation of the Department of Homeland Security, contending that a radical centralization of government agencies is necessary to fight terrorism. Ron Paul claims that such a reorganization will actually make America more vulnerable to terrorists by diverting resources away from antiterrorist activities to rearrange government offices. Does the fact that George W. Bush is president of the United States make his argument automatically more convincing than representative Paul's? Explain.

4. Samuel Francis contends that America should close its borders because mass immigration has created safe havens for terrorists to hide. In contrast, Daniel T. Griswold claims that restricting immigration will not make America safer because terrorists do not enter the United States as immigrants, but on temporary tourist and student visas. How do you think Francis would respond to Griswold's argument? Do you think he would change his mind about closing America's borders given the facts that

Griswold provides? Please explain, citing from Francis's viewpoint to develop your answer.

Chapter 4

1. Nick Gillespie contends that trading freedom and privacy for enhanced security will lead to ever-increasing restrictions on civil liberties. In contrast, Richard A. Posner argues in favor of such a trade, claiming that the September 11, 2001, terrorist attacks illustrate the need for extra security. Write an essay on the balance between civil liberties and national security, devoting one paragraph to the benefits of enhancing security and another to protecting civil liberties. Cite from both viewpoints to develop your lists and add any other items you can think of. Finally, write a conclusion in favor of security or civil liberties, providing sound reasons for your choice.

2. Patricia J. Williams maintains that ethnic profiling is ineffective because an individual's physical characteristics do not always convey his or her intention to commit a terrorist act. Bruce J. Terris argues in favor of ethnic profiling, claiming that targeting those most likely to commit terrorist acts—Arabs—improves the chance that future terrorist acts can be prevented. Do you think that Arab Americans and visiting Middle Easterners should accept increased scrutiny and interrogation by U.S. officials? Explain why or why not.

3. According to John Derbyshire, a mandatory national ID card would destroy the freedoms that define America. On the other hand, Margaret Carlson claims that such a card would help U.S. officials combat terrorism. Based on the readings, what kinds of things might the government learn about individuals if a national ID card were mandatory? In what way might this information in the hands of government hurt U.S. citizens? Do you think that Derbyshire's concerns are founded, or is Carlson right that an ID card is needed to combat terrorism? Please explain.

Organizations to Contact

The editors have compiled the following list of organizations concerned with the issues debated in this book. The descriptions are derived from materials provided by the organizations. All have publications or information available for interested readers. The list was compiled on the date of publication of the present volume; the information provided here may change. Be aware that many organizations take several weeks or longer to respond to inquiries, so allow as much time as possible.

American Civil Liberties Union (ACLU)
125 Broad St., 18th Floor, New York, NY 10004-2400
(212) 549-2500
e-mail: aclu@aclu.org • website: www.aclu.org
The American Civil Liberties Union is a national organization that works to defend Americans' civil rights guaranteed by the U.S. Constitution, arguing that measures to protect national security should not compromise fundamental civil liberties. It publishes and distributes policy statements, pamphlets, and press releases with titles such as "In Defense of Freedom in a Time of Crisis" and "National ID Cards: 5 Reasons Why They Should Be Rejected."

American Enterprise Institute (AEI)
1150 17th St. NW, Washington, DC 20036
(202) 862-5800 • (202) 862-7177
website: www.aei.org
The American Enterprise Institute for Public Policy Research is a scholarly research institute that is dedicated to preserving limited government, private enterprise, and a strong foreign policy and national defense. It publishes books, including *Study of Revenge: The First World Trade Center Attack* and *Saddam Hussein's War Against America*. Articles about terrorism and September 11 can be found in its magazine, *American Enterprise*, and on its website.

American Friends Service Committee (AFSC)
1501 Cherry St., Philadelphia, PA 19102
(215) 241-7000 • fax: (215) 241-7275
e-mail: afscinfo@afsc.org • website: www.afsc.org
The American Friends Service Committee is a Quaker organization that includes people of various faiths who are committed to social justice, peace, and humanitarian service. Its work is based on the Religious Society of Friends (Quaker) belief in the worth of ev-

ery person, and faith in the power of love to overcome violence and injustice. Founded in 1917 to provide conscientious objectors with an opportunity to aid civilian victims during World War I, today the AFSC has programs that focus on issues related to economic justice, peace-building and demilitarization, social justice, and youth, in the United States, and in Africa, Asia, Europe, Latin America, the Middle East, and at the United Nations. The organization publishes the newsletter *Faultlines*, and other periodicals, including *Peacework*, *Toward Peace and Justice*, and the *Quaker Service Bulletin*. It also makes available on its website the Youth and Militarism Online Magazine.

The Brookings Institution

1775 Massachusetts Ave. NW, Washington, DC 20036
(202) 797-6000 • fax: (202) 797-6004
e-mail: brookinfo@brook.edu • website: www.brookings.org

The institution, founded in 1927, is a think tank that conducts research and education in foreign policy, economics, government, and the social sciences. In 2001 it began America's Response to Terrorism, a project that provides briefings and analysis to the public and which is featured on the center's website. Other publications include the quarterly *Brookings Review*, periodic *Policy Briefs*, and books including *Terrorism and U.S. Foreign Policy*.

Cato Institute

1000 Massachusetts Ave. NW, Washington, DC 20001-5403
(202) 842-0200 • fax: (202) 842-3490
e-mail: cato@cato.org • website: www.cato.org

The institute is a nonpartisan public policy research foundation dedicated to limiting the role of government and protecting individual liberties. It publishes the quarterly magazine *Regulation*, the bimonthly *Cato Policy Report*, and numerous policy papers and articles. Works on terrorism include "Does U.S. Intervention Overseas Breed Terrorism?" and "Military Tribunals No Answer."

Center for Defense Information

1779 Massachusetts Ave. NW, Suite 615, Washington, DC 20036
(202) 332-0600 • fax: (202) 462-4559
e-mail: info@cdi.org • website: www.cdi.org

The Center for Defense Information is a nonpartisan, nonprofit organization that researches all aspects of global security. It seeks to educate the public and policy makers about issues such as weapons systems, security policy, and defense budgeting. It publishes the monthly publication *Defense Monitor*, the issue brief

"National Missile Defense: What Does It All Mean?" and the studies "Homeland Security: A Competitive Strategies Approach" and "Reforging the Sword."

Center for Immigration Studies
1522 K St. NW, Suite 820, Washington, DC 20005-1202
(202) 466-8185 • fax: (202) 466-8076
e-mail: center@cis.org • website: www.cis.org

The Center for Immigration Studies is the nation's only think tank dedicated to research and analysis of the economic, social, and demographic impacts of immigration on the United States. An independent, nonpartisan, nonprofit research organization founded in 1985, the center aims to expand public support for an immigration policy that is both pro-immigrant and low-immigration. Among its publications are the backgrounders "The USA PATRIOT Act of 2001: A Summary of the Anti-Terrorism Law's Immigration-Related Provisions" and "America's Identity Crisis: Document Fraud Is Pervasive and Pernicious."

Central Intelligence Agency (CIA)
Office of Public Affairs, Washington, DC 20505
(703) 482-0623 • fax: (703) 482-1739
website: www.cia.gov

The CIA was created in 1947 with the signing of the National Security Act (NSA) by President Harry S. Truman. The NSA charged the Director of Central Intelligence (DCI) with coordinating the nation's intelligence activities and correlating, evaluating, and disseminating intelligence that affects national security. The CIA is an independent agency, responsible to the president through the DCI, and accountable to the American people through the Intelligence Oversight Committee of the U.S. Congress. Publications, including *Factbook on Intelligence*, are available on its website.

Chemical and Biological Arms Control Institute (CBACI)
1747 Pennsylvania Ave. NW, 7th Floor, Washington, DC 20006
(202) 296-3550 • fax: (202) 296-3574
e-mail: cbaci@cbaci.org • website: www.cbaci.org

CBACI is a nonprofit corporation that promotes arms control and nonproliferation, with particular focus on the elimination of chemical and biological weapons. It fosters this goal by drawing on an extensive international network to provide an innovative program of research, analysis, technical support, and education. Among the institute's publications is the bimonthly report *Dispatch* and the reports "Bioterrorism in the United States: Threat, Preparedness, and Response" and "Contagion and Conflict: Health as a Global Security Challenge."

Federal Bureau of Investigation (FBI)

935 Pennsylvania Ave. NW, Room 7972, Washington, DC 20535
(202) 324-3000
website: www.fbi.gov

The FBI, the principle investigative arm of the U.S. Department of Justice, evolved from an unnamed force of Special Agents formed on July 26, 1909. It has the authority and responsibility to investigate specific crimes assigned to it. The FBI also is authorized to provide other law enforcement agencies with cooperative services, such as fingerprint identification, laboratory examinations, and police training. The mission of the FBI is to uphold the law through the investigation of violations of federal criminal law; to protect the United States from foreign intelligence and terrorist activities; to provide leadership and law enforcement assistance to federal, state, local, and international agencies; and to perform these responsibilites in a manner that is responsive to the needs of the public and is faithful to the Constitution of the United States. Press releases, congressional statements, and major speeches on issues concerning the FBI are available on the agency's website.

Henry L. Stimson Center

11 Dupont Circle NW, 9th Floor, Washington, DC 20036
(202) 223-5956 • fax: (202) 238-9604
website: www.stimson.org

The Stimson Center is an independent public policy institute committed to finding and promoting innovative solutions to the security challenges confronting the United States and other nations. The center directs the Chemical and Biological Weapons Nonproliferation Project, which serves as a clearinghouse of information related to the monitoring and implementation of the 1972 Biological Weapons Convention. The center produces reports, papers, and books on policy and biological and other weapons of mass destruction.

Institute for Policy Studies (IPS)

733 15th St. NW, Suite 1020, Washington, DC 20005
(202) 234-9382 • fax: (202) 387-7915
website: www.ips-dc.org

The Institute for Policy Studies is a progressive think tank that works to develop societies built around the values of justice and nonviolence. It publishes reports including *Global Perspectives: A Media Guide to Foreign Policy Experts.* Numerous articles and interviews on September 11 and terrorism are available on its website.

National Security Agency
9800 Savage Road, Ft. Meade, MD 20755-6248
(301) 688-6524
website: www.nsa.gov

The National Security Agency coordinates, directs, and performs activities, such as designing cipher systems, which protects American information systems and produces foreign intelligence information. It is the largest employer of mathematicians in the United States and also hires the nation's best codemakers and codebreakers. Speeches, briefings, and reports are available at the website.

United States Department of State, Counterterrorism Office
Office of Public Affairs, Room 2507
U.S. Department of State
2201 C St. NW, Washington, DC 20520
(202) 647-4000
e-mail: secretary@state.gov • website: www.state.gov/s/ct

The office works to develop and implement American counterterrorism strategy and to improve cooperation with foreign governments. Articles and speeches by government officials are available on its website.

Washington Institute for Near East Policy
1828 L St. NW, Suite 1050, Washington, DC 20036
(202) 452-0650 • fax: (202) 223-5364
e-mail: info@washingtoninstitute.org
website: washingtoninstitute.org

The institute is an independent organization that produces research and analysis on the Middle East and U.S. policy in the region. It publishes numerous position papers and reports on Middle Eastern politics and social developments. It also publishes position papers on Middle Eastern military issues and U.S. policy, including "The Future of Iraq," and "Building for Peace: An American Strategy for the Middle East."

Bibliography of Books

Robert Baer

See No Evil: The True Story of a Ground Soldier in the CIA's War on Terrorism. New York: Crown Publishers, 2002.

Wendy Barnaby

The Plague Makers: The Secret World of Biological Warfare. New York: Random House, 1999.

Richard Butler

Fatal Choice: Nuclear Weapons and the Illusion of Missile Defense. Boulder, CO: Westview, 2001.

Richard Butler

The Greatest Threat: Iraq, Weapons of Mass Destruction, and the Growing Crisis in Global Security. New York: PublicAffairs, 2000.

Kurt M. Campbell and Michèle A. Flourney

To Prevail: An American Strategy for the Campaign Against Terrorism. Washington, DC: CSIS Press, 2001.

Cabel Carr

The Lessons of Terror: A History of Warfare Against Civilizations: Why It Has Always Failed and Why It Will Fail Again. New York: Random House, 2002.

Anthony H. Cordesman

Strategic Threats and National Missile Defense: Defending the U.S. Homeland. Westport, CT: Praeger, 2002.

Anthony H. Cordesman

Terrorism, Asymmetric Warfare, and Weapons of Mass Destruction: Defending the U.S. Homeland. Westport, CT: Praeger, 2002.

Eric Croddy et al.

Chemical and Biological Warfare: A Comprehensive Guide for the Concerned Citizen. New York: Copernicus Books, 2002.

James X. Dempsey and David Cole

Terrorism and the Constitution: Sacrificing Civil Liberties in the Name of National Security. Washington, DC: First Amendment Foundation, 2002.

Craig Eisendrath, ed.

National Insecurity: U.S. Intelligence After the Cold War. Philadelphia: Temple University Press, 2000.

Steven Emerson

American Jihad: The Terrorists Living Among Us. New York: Free Press, 2002.

Peter D. Feaver and Richard H. Kohn, eds.

Soldiers and Civilians: The Civil-Military Gap and American National Security. Cambridge, MA: MIT Press, 2001.

Harold A. Feiveson and Bruce G. Blair, eds.

The Nuclear Turning Point: A Blueprint for Deep Cuts and De-Alerting of Nuclear Weapons. Washington, DC: Brookings Institution Press, 1999.

| William H. Frist | *When Every Moment Counts: What You Need to Know About Bioterrorism from the Senate's Only Doctor.* Lanham, MD: Rowman & Littlefield, 2002. |

| Roger Handberg | *Ballistic Missile Defense and the Future of American Security.* Westport, CT: Praeger, 2002. |

| Katrina Vanden Heuvel, ed. | *A Just Response: The Nation on Terrorism, Democracy, and September 11, 2001.* New York: Thunder Mouth Press, 2002. |

| James F. Hoge and Gideon Rose, eds. | *How Did This Happen?: Terrorism and the New War.* New York: PublicAffairs, 2001. |

| James M. Lindsay and Michael E. O'Hanlon | *Defending America: The Case for Limited National Missile Defense.* Washington, DC: Brookings Institution Press, 2001. |

| Rajul Mahajan | *The New Crusade: America's War on Terrorism.* New York: Monthly Review Press, 2002. |

| Philip M. Melanson | *Secrecy Wars: National Security, Privacy, and the Public's Right to Know.* Washington, DC: Brassey's, 2001. |

| Paul R. Pillar | *Terrorism and U.S. Foreign Policy.* Washington, DC: Brookings Institution Press, 2001. |

| Daniel Pipes | *Militant Islam Reaches America.* New York: W.W. Norton, 2002. |

| Jeffrey T. Richelson | *The Wizards of Langley: Inside the CIA's Directorate of Science and Technology.* Boulder, CO: Westview Press, 2002. |

| Tom Sauer | *Nuclear Arms Control: Nuclear Deterrence in the Post–Cold War Period.* New York: St. Martin's, 1998. |

| Phil Scranton, ed. | *Beyond September 11: An Anthology of Dissent.* Sterling, VA: Pluto Press, 2002. |

| Robert David Steele | *On Intelligence: Spies and Secrecy in an Open World.* Fairfax, VA: AFCEA International Press, 2000. |

| Strobe Talbott and Nayan Chanda, eds. | *The Age of Terror: America and the World After September 11.* New York: Basic Books, 2001. |

| Raymond Tanter | *Rogue Regimes: Terrorism and Proliferation.* New York: St. Martin's Press, 1998. |

| Howard Zinn | *Terrorism and War.* New York: Seven Stories Press, 2002. |

| Stephen Zunes | *Tinder Box: U.S. Middle East Policy and the Roots of Terrorism.* Monroe, ME: Common Courage Press, 2002. |

Index